BIRMINGHAM COLLEGE OF FOOD, TOURISM & CREATIVE STUDIES
COLLEGE LIBRARY, SUMMER ROW
BIRMINGHAM B3 1JB
Tel: (0121) 243 0055

MANAGING

WINE AND WINE SALES

Series in Tourism and Hospitality Management

Series Editors:

Professor Roy C. Wood
The Scottish Hotel School, University of Strathclyde, UK

Stephen J. Page
Massey University, New Zealand

Series Consultant:

Professor C. L. Jenkins
The Scottish Hotel School, University of Strathclyde, UK

Textbooks in this series:

Behavioural Studies in Hospitality Management
R. Carmouche and N. Kelly
ISBN 0 412 60850 2, 232 pages

Managing Human Resources in the European Tourism and Hospitality Industry
A strategic approach
T. Baum
ISBN 0 412 55630 8, 280 pages

Interpersonal Skills for Hospitality Management
M. A. Clark
ISBN 0 412 57330 X, 232 pages

Hospitality and Tourism Law
M. Poustie, N. Geddes, W. Stewart and J. Ross
ISBN 0 412 62080 4, 320 pages

Business Accounting for Hospitality and Tourism
H. Atkinson, A. Berry and R. Jarvis
ISBN 0 412 48080 8, 432 pages

Economics for Hospitality Management
P. Cullen
ISBN 0 412 608540 6, 224 pages

Tourism in the Pacific
C. Michael Hall and Stephen J. Page
ISBN 0 412 12500 6, 304 pages

Managing Wine and Wine Sales
J. E. Fattorini
ISBN 0 412 72190 2, 200 pages

Marketing Tourism, Hospitality and Leisure in Europe
S. Horner and J. Swarbrooke
ISBN 0 412 62170 3, 736 pages

Managing Packaged Tourism
E. Laws
ISBN 0 415 11347 4, ca. 224 pages

Research Methods in Hospitality and Tourism
M. Clark, M. Riley, E. Wilkie and R. C. Wood
ISBN 1 861 52046 8, ca. 192 pages

The Business of Rural Tourism
D. Getz and S. Page
ISBN 0 415 13511 7, ca. 192 pages

Human Resource Management for Hospitality Services
A. Goldsmith, D. Nickson, D. Sloan and R. C. Wood
ISBN 1 861 52095 6, ca. 224 pages

Hospitality Accounting, 5th edn
R. Kotas and M. Conlan
ISBN 1 861 52086 7, ca. 352 pages

Tourism Marketing
L. Lumsdon
ISBN 1 861 52045 X, ca. 304 pages

Tourism in Scotland
R. Maclellan and R. Smith, eds
ISBN 1 861 52089 1, ca. 304 pages

Tourism in Developing Countries
M. Opperman
ISBN 0 415 13939 2, ca. 192 pages

Corporate Strategies in Tourism
J. Tribe
ISBN 0 415 14204 0, ca. 240 pages

Working in Hotels and Catering, 2nd edn
R. C. Wood
ISBN 0 415 13881 7, ca. 224 pages

Tourism: An Introduction
R. Youell
ISBN 0 415 13185 5, ca. 304 pages

Books in this series are available on free inspection for lecturers considering the texts for course adoption. Details of these and any other International Thomson Business Press titles are available by writing to the publishers (Berkshire House, 168-173 High Holborn, London WC1V 7AA) or by telephoning the Promotions Department on 0171 497 1422.

MANAGING WINE AND WINE SALES

J.E. FATTORINI

UNIVERSITY OF STRATHCLYDE, UK

INTERNATIONAL THOMSON BUSINESS PRESS
I(T)P® An International Thomson Publishing Company

London • Bonn • Boston • Johannesburg • Madrid • Melbourne • Mexico City • New York • Paris
Singapore • Tokyo • Toronto • Albany, NY • Belmont, CA • Cincinnati, OH • Detroit, MI

Managing Wine and Wine Sales

Copyright ©1997 J.E. Fattorini

First published by International Thomson Business Press

I(T)P® A division of International Thomson Publishing Inc.
The ITP logo is a trademark under licence

All rights reserved. No part of this work which is copyright may be reproduced or used in any form or by any means – graphic, electronic, or mechanical, including photocopying, recording, taping or information storage and retrieval systems – without the written permission of the Publisher, except in accordance with the provisions of the Copyright Designs and Patents Act 1988.

Whilst the Publisher has taken all reasonable care in the preparation of this book the Publisher makes no representation, express or implied, with regard to the accuracy of the information contained in this book and cannot accept any legal responsibility or liability for any errors or omissions from the book or the consequences thereof.

Products and services that are referred to in this book may be either trademarks and/or registered trademarks of their respective owners. The Publisher/s and Author/s make no claim to these trademarks.

British Library Cataloguing-in-Publication Data
A catalogue record for this book is available from the British Library

First edition 1997

Typeset by Hodgson Williams Associates, Tunbridge Wells and Cambridge
Printed in the UK by the Alden Press, Oxford

ISBN 0-412-72190-2

International Thomson Business Press
Berkshire House
168–173 High Holborn
London WC1V 7AA
UK

International Thomson Business Press
20 Park Plaza
13th Floor
Boston MA 02116
USA

http://www.itbp.com

Contents

Series Editors' Foreword xi
Acknowledgements xiii
Introduction xv

PART 1 WINE CONSUMPTION

1. The development of wine in the hotel and restaurant sector 3
Introduction 3
Fifty years of change in the wine trade 5
The need for more highly trained staff 10
Wine and restaurants in the future 13
Summary 18
Questions and exercises 18
Further reading 19

2. The modern wine consumer 20
Introduction 20
Who drinks what? 21
New consumer attitudes towards wine 29
Questions and exercises 36
Further reading 36

PART 2 SELECTION, PURCHASING AND CONTROL

3. Choosing wines for a restaurant 41
Introduction 41
Sensory evaluation of wines 42
The question of relative worth 48
The commercial viability of wines 51
Conclusion 56
Questions and exercises 56
Further reading 57

4. Purchasing wine ... 58
Introduction ... 58
Supply structure ... 59
Supplier selection ... 63
Developing a supplier policy ... 67
Questions and exercises ... 68
Further reading ... 68

5. Beverage control ... 70
Introduction ... 70
Issues in beverage control ... 71
Wine stock control systems ... 73
Performance measures ... 77
Wine pricing ... 80
Summary ... 83
Questions and exercises ... 84
Further reading ... 84

PART 3 WINES IN THE RESTAURANT

6. Developing a wine list ... 87
Introduction ... 87
Writing the wine list ... 88
Practical considerations ... 94
The wine list and the consumer ... 95
Marketing research ... 96
Summary ... 100
Questions and exercises ... 101
Further reading ... 101

7. Merchandising wine ... 102
Introduction ... 102
They know everything but what it tastes like ... 102
Innovative ways of selling wine ... 104
Creating a merchandising strategy ... 111
Alternatives to straightforward wine list sales ... 113
Summary ... 119
Questions and exercises ... 120
Further reading ... 120

8. Wine service skills ... 121
Introduction ... 121
The process of wine service ... 121
Theatricality in wine service ... 133
Dealing with disasters ... 135
Training in wine service ... 135
Questions and exercises ... 135
Further reading ... 136

9. Training specialist staff 137
Introduction 137
The sommelier 137
Development of product knowledge and service skills 138
Wine training and education 141
Basic training 141
Intermediate training 144
Advanced training 148
Super advanced training 151
Questions and exercises 152
Further reading. 153

10. Wine books and periodicals 154
Introduction 154
Books 155
Periodicals 157

Bibliography 159

Index 163

For C

Series Editors' Foreword

The International Thomson Business Press Series in Tourism and Hospitality Management is dedicated to the publication of high quality textbooks and other volumes that will be of benefit to those engaged in tourism, hotel and hospitality education, especially at degree and postgraduate level. The series has two principal strands: core textbooks on key areas of the curriculum; and the Topics in Tourism and Hospitality series which includes highly focused and shorter texts on particular themes and issues. All the authors in the series are experts in their own fields, actively engaged in teaching, research and consultancy in tourism and hospitality. Each book comprises an authoritative blend of subject-relevant theoretical considerations and practical applications. Furthermore, a unique quality of the series is that it is student oriented, offering accessible texts that take account of the realities of administration, management and operations in tourism and hospitality contexts, being constructively critical without losing sight of the overall goal of providing clear accounts of essential concepts, issues and techniques.

The series is committed to quality, accessibility, relevance and originality in its approach. Quality is ensured as a result of a vigorous refereeing process, unusual in the publication of textbooks. Accessibility is achieved through the use of innovative textual design techniques, and the use of discussion points, case studies and exercises within books, all geared to encouraging a comprehensive understanding of the material contained therein. Relevance and originality together result from the experience of authors as key authorities in their fields.

The tourism and hospitality industries are diverse and dynamic industries and it is the intention of the editors to reflect this diversity and dynamism by publishing quality texts that enhance topical subjects without losing sight of enduring themes. The Series Editors and Consultant are grateful to Steven Reed of International Thomson Business Press for his commitment, expertise and support of this philosophy.

Series Editors
Stephen J. Page
Massey University – Albany
Auckland
New Zealand

Professor Roy C. Wood
The Scottish Hotel School
University of Strathclyde
United Kingdom

Series Consultant
Professor C. L. Jenkins
The Scottish Hotel School
University of Strathclyde
United Kingdom

Acknowledgements

I owe a special debt of gratitude to my parents and Professor Roy Wood who have provided support, advice and occasional coercion throughout this project. Bob and Eileen Wright of the Wright Wine Company in Skipton deserve special thanks for their great help during much of the writing, and I only hope that what they read here does justice to what they taught me. A host of others have freely given their advice or in other ways contributed to this book: Dennis Watkins of the Angel Inn at Hetton; Andy Kemp, David Moore and Malcolm Ogilvie of Oddbins; Bill Laverick of Wine Rack, York; Toni Alberti and Gianfranco Bucher of the Grand Hotel Villa Serbelloni, Bellagio; Albert Lord. It seems fitting to thank those whose ready corkscrew has so frequently been on hand to provide inspiration at various stages, not least Richard Wilkins and Julian Kaye. Some of the less austere parts of this text may date back to flashes of 'creativity' in their company. Finally I would like to thank Caroline for her patience, and calm encouragement.

Introduction

During the writing of this book many people have been keen to tell me how lucky I am to have the chance to write a book about wine. The assumption, and I think it is an understable one, is that in order to write a book about wine you need to drink a great deal of it. This assumption would seem to stem from the fact that the vast majority of wine books are about *consumption* and for the most part are aimed at *consumers*.

This book, I am sorry to tell, does not deal with consumption. The last thing wine consumers need from me is a book telling them what to drink and how. Any trip to a bookshop will tell you that there is quite enough on this subject already, written by those far more qualified than me. What consumers do need though are restaurateurs, wine bar managers, publicans, licensed retailers, in fact all those who *sell* wine, to be experts in *how* to sell wine well.

The last twenty years or so have seen an unprecedented democratization of wine consumption and many who would never have considered drinking wine in the past now regularly do so. It is no longer the preserve of the middle class or, at least if it is, we now have a middle class that encompasses far more than it did before. Wine is now available from a whole variety of outlets. Perhaps the most important new wine outlets are the supermarkets which have changed our perception of wine from a special and rare treat to an everyday commodity. For those selling wine this poses both an opportunity and a threat. A larger and more discriminating market means that there is a great deal of money to be made by selling wine, whether for consumption in the home or at a restaurant. The threat comes from the fact that as consumers drink wine in a variety of outlets they will inevitably become more demanding customers and will gravitate towards those that offer both value for money and 'added value' in the form of better service. The old image of the supercilious sommelier selling warm Liebfraumilch and Southern European gut-rot is well and truly out. The new wine consumer wants quality, good value wine and practical, honest wine service.

This book describes the modern consumers and then outlines how to satisfy them from the particular viewpoint of the hotel and restaurant industry. The concentration on the hotel and restaurant sector is for two reasons. First, the book is aimed at students on hospitality management courses and practising hotel and restaurant managers. Second, the other wine sales sector, licensed retailers, have a far simpler relationship with wine. They are concerned with selling the bottle, not serving it as part of the holistic experience of a meal. In addition, they are in many ways more sophisticated in their sales techniques and have more to teach than learn from the hotel and restaurant sector. This is perhaps a product of the structure of the modern wine retailing industry where the most important players, supermarkets and high street chains, belong to large groups who can afford the market research that is beyond older, independent merchants.

The text is divided up into three parts. Part 1 outlines the changes that have taken place in wine consumption in the last twenty or so years followed by an analysis of the modern wine consumer. The main thrust of the changes in recent years has been that customers are becoming more adventurous and consequently more demanding. They have higher expectations and so to satisfy these expectations properly, those who sell wine must understand them and work to meet them.

Part 2 covers the selection and purchase of wine. In the past restaurateurs have only had the confidence to carry out this task if they were avid wine consumers themselves. Often they have left the selection of wines to their merchant. While most merchants would carry out this task to the best of their ability, they do not own the restaurant. The restaurateur knows the food best and they are the ones who have to take responsibility for their wine list.

One of the reasons that restaurateurs leave wine selection up to their merchants is because of the rather haphazard and complicated structure of the wine trade. In Chapter 4 this is briefly outlined to allow the reader to understand better who is who and where they are likely to get the best deal. This chapter also examines what services and benefits to look for when selecting a merchant or merchants. Finally in Part 2, Chapter 5 examines beverage control. Although similar in structure to any other form of produce control, issues of perishability, pilferage and money tied up in idle stock make good beverage control a specialized and important skill.

Part 3, wines in the restaurant, covers the marketing and selling skills necessary to develop wine sales successfully. The most important tool in successful wine sales, the wine list, is discussed in Chapter 6. This chapter complements what was covered in Chapter 3 on the selection and purchase of wine, giving gastronomic and practical considerations in the development of a good wine list.

With the wine list written, many restaurateurs leave their wine merchandising at that. However, Chapter 7 gives a range of other ways to 'sell' wine, from specific incentives to buy such as celebrity endorsements to developing a 'winey' atmosphere in the restaurant. Also covered here is the subject of wine by the glass, a rapidly developing form of wine sales which if done properly is a way of earning a good margin.

Chapters 8 and 9 show how to make the best use of the most underutilized tool in wine sales, the staff. Chapter 8 covers wine service and I have taken the opportunity to recommend an informal and ultimately flexible service style. There are two reasons for this. First, this book is aimed at the whole range of modern restaurants from the most formal, old-fashioned restaurant to the modern, continental style brasserie or public house. Ultimately wine service should fit into the overall style of the outlet and hopefully this is the general message of the chapter. Second, customers appear to prefer a more relaxed and informal style of wine service as they become more frequent wine consumers. Drinking wine is no longer the treat it once was. When customers are drinking wine every day at home, they want to treat it informally when they are out in restaurants. Chapter 9 covers staff training. Curiously, in a time when wine service is becoming more relaxed and informal, staff need to be better trained. More knowledgeable customers are more likely to ask searching questions and want to go to restaurants where the staff know what they are talking about. This chapter develops a staff training programme around the framework of the Wine and Spirit Education Trust examinations as they form a useful framework of product knowledge development and are widely recognized, although the programme could be fashioned around a variety of similar qualifications.

Finally in Chapter 10 there is a brief review of a number of influential wine books, concentrating particularly on those of use to restaurateurs. As I mentioned earlier, the vast majority of wine books deal with wine *consumption* as opposed to sales. This does not mean that these consumer oriented texts are of no value, but that when reading them one should be aware of the market for which they are written.

With the principal market of students in mind this text has been written with a series of end-of-chapter exercises and questions. For lecturers these could form the basis of in-class exercises and assignments, giving rather more variety to beverage management classes than pure product knowledge tests. A number of them could also be used by practising restaurateurs to develop the sales skills and knowledge of staff in their own outlet.

Wine consumption — PART 1

Part 1

Wine consumption

The development of wine in the hotel and restaurant sector 1

> **Key concepts**
>
> The main concepts covered in this chapter are:
> - fifty years of change in Britain's wine trade;
> - specialist staff training;
> - wine and restaurants in the future.

INTRODUCTION

Britain is in an a unique position in the world of wine. We produce very little and while many go to great lengths to promote what is produced, the country's northern, wet, cloudy climate prevents it from becoming a major wine exporter. Yet despite having a very limited commercial wine-producing industry of its own, Britain is currently, and has been for a very long time, a major trader in wine, to the extent that it is often referred to as the centre of the world wine trade. Cities such as London, Edinburgh and Bristol have for many years been used by wine producers from around the world (just look at the establishment dates of some of their merchants). In many of the most famous wine-producing regions, among the names of local producers, British names also appear on bottles, Taylor, Warre and Graham in the port-producing Douro valley, Barton and Palmer in Bordeaux.

All this points to the very long-standing status of Britain as a trader in wine and the regard with which its merchants and general expertise are held in producer nations. Yet none of this has prepared either Britain's wine trade or consuming public for what has widely been regarded as a revolution in wine production and consumption in the last fifty years. This revolution is not confined to changes that merely affect us in Britain—in many respects the changes in very traditional producer nations such as France or Italy have been more wide ranging. Both these countries are finding that the younger generation is moving away from domestically produced wines to imported beers and spirits. In Italy, Irish theme pubs selling stout are expanding at an astonishing rate. In Spain fashionable young men no longer drink wine on an evening out, but buy a prestigious brand of Scotch whisky to share. In Britain, despite a long history of involvement in the wine trade and even a history of wine consumption throughout the population (Barr, 1995), by the end of World War II wine consumption was a regular pleasure for the few and an occasional treat for rather more. In comparison to the situation today the difference is huge.

This chapter gives an overview of those changes and how they affect the restaurateur today. It is not an in-depth examination of the development of the trade, as this has been done with great style in a number of other books (Driver, 1983; Johnson, 1989). The aim is to take a number of key changes and point out how they have affected the wine sales function of restaurants both then and now. Initially the chapter discusses changes that have affected the public's perception of wine. Enjoyment of wine has been transformed from something of a minority pursuit, given an image of snobbery often leading to stereotypical images of both those who are keen on wine and those who attempt to sell it, to a regular part of life for many in Britain.

The theme of snobbery is often at the heart of changes in wine consumption. This has been evident in the rise to prominence of so-called 'New World' wine-producing nations. Initially led by Australia and the USA, the New World now comprises an impressive list of nations from South America, Eastern Europe and Southern Africa, some totally new to wine production and some returning to the world stage with revitalized industries. The importance of these countries is discussed, as are changes in the home market. The change in wine from a regular drink for the few (often characterized by the 'wine snob' label) with the rest only enjoying it on special celebratory occasions, to a regular drink for many is discussed in rather more depth, together with the ramifications for those who sell wine, not least hoteliers and restaurateurs.

The chapter then examines a very practical area in terms of wine sales, the need for increasingly broad knowledge in those who sell wine, both staff and management. A knowledgeable public, accustomed to buying wine from off-licences and wine merchants, can no longer be persuaded to spend outrageous amounts of money on wines they may well have seen on a shop shelf for half or two-thirds of the price on a wine list. The diners are becoming more expert consumers of restaurant services and need treating with increased respect.

Finally, the chapter examines the way in which the market is likely to change in coming years. As restaurant customers see wine as an everyday commodity, the policy of using the large profit margin on wine as a way of subsidising the minimal profits on food sales and covering overheads will come under increasing pressure. Furthermore, what will those factors beyond the control of the restaurateurs have on wine sales. Massive duty differentials, particularly between Britain and France, make the price of restaurant wine look very unattractive. While many may buy it, they will resent the feeling of being a captive market, paying £8.00 or £9.00 for a vin de pays which they know is available in France for £1.50.

FIFTY YEARS OF CHANGE IN THE WINE TRADE

The importance of history

In the UK wine trade it is hard to get away from the concept of time passing and the nobility of age. Most of the best regarded merchants have long-established businesses tracing their origins back to the eighteenth century or even earlier. Few wine textbooks can avoid the temptation of starting with a historical view of the subject country or region. Even the British view of wines is unique when it comes to age – the concept of the prized cellar filled with ancient dusty bottles maturing into a vinous senility is a strong one. All too often these ancient wines are kept for so many years that they are long past their finest hour. They are then drunk by those who imagine that enjoying the insipid vinegary taste will somehow come with (occasional) practice, rather like teenagers attempting to gag down the first attempt at their parents' Scotch whisky. This is not to belittle those wines that live for fifty even a hundred years, instead it is an example of the importance of age in the wine trade.

Such a jaundiced view is not to deprecate in any way the enviable historical position and development of Britain's wine trade. Royal marriages, international treaties, the power of empire, good fortune and sheer hard work all played their part. (See Johnson, 1989 for an outstanding history of the development of wine and the wine trade.) What is remarkable about the British wine trade is that the history of the business, and all the romantic associations that accompany its long establishment, enhanced its status to a level that is often envied by those trying to merchandise more mundane items.

Why we favour who we do

A knowledge of the historical foundations of the wine trade is often useful in understanding why certain countries feature so strongly on our wine lists today, while others producing similar quantities of quality wine hardly credit a mention. When dealing with the British love of claret few wine books can avoid at least a passing reference to the marriage of Henry Plantagenet of Anjou, later Henry II of England, to Eleanor of Aquitaine. The trade of English wool in return for Aquitaine wines (especially what we now know as claret), which was assisted by the royal marriage, started a passion that exists to the present day. Similarly the Methuen treaty, with its preferential tariffs on Portuguese wines, led to that other mainstay of the traditional British wine list, port, becoming a national favourite.

Britain's imperial past has also affected what it drinks. Australia is now best known for light, fruit-driven styles and the innovative use of oak. Although often thought of as a relative newcomer to wine production, its roots in the export of wine to the UK can be traced back to the production of heavy, sweet and fortified wines that enjoyed the benefit of lower tariffs which were part of the Imperial Preference System. This was withdrawn when the UK joined the European Community, and Australia suffered a period of decline until the mid-1980s when a weak Australian dollar made Australian wine competitive again. The wine drinking public took to the lighter, fruitier style which was different from that generally produced in Europe.

Thus from these examples one can see how wines come in and out of favour. It is a myth that wines are 'discovered' by wine journalists or buyers in dark, mould-covered cellars. Government treaties and exchange rate fluctuations bring wines in and out of fashion, but do not evoke the public's imagination until they have become historical events of several hundred years ago.

The changing face of wine selling

Before the removal of personal allowances for bringing wines and spirits into the UK from overseas, those who wanted to buy wine in Britain had two options. They could buy wine when dining in restaurants, where they often had to pay very high prices (albeit without much of an idea of what to compare them with since until recently this was often the only occasion upon which wine was drunk). Alternatively, they could go to a wine retailer – an off-licence or wine merchant. I make the distinction because although in legal terms they were both licensed to sell the same products for consumption off the premises, wine merchants and off-licences were invariably very different classes of shop. A particularly good description of an off-licence in 'the bad old days' before Britain's revolution in wine-drinking habits was given to me by a very experienced area manager with one of the country's largest drinks retailers. He described how the off-licence manager, a man in his fifties, would spend his days at work sitting on a stool in the doorway between the shop and his back office. Shambling down from the company flat upstairs, still in his slippers, a grubby shirt and cardigan, his days were spent smoking on his stool and chatting with friends who came into the shop, while sales assistants filled shelves and his wife made tea and did her knitting in the back. He had never drunk wine in his life, enjoying only beer and whisky and always keeping a bottle open in the back. Yet remarkably he was not an oddity. Throughout the company's estate, managers of wine shops viewed wine with the same disregard.

Wine merchants have always been an altogether different style of shop. The merchant's adage that 'to make a small fortune in the wine trade, you need a large one to start with', often meant that those with considerable personal wealth were involved. The very middle-class image of wine merchants has also been enhanced by the type of young men (usually) who worked in them. They were often characterized as public school boys who were not clever enough for the Army and City, yet not pious enough for the Cloth. Not surprisingly, this has all affected the public view of wine and the wine trade. Unless they came from backgrounds similar to those who patronised the wine merchants, many felt excluded and uncomfortable in the traditional shops. This discomfort was often compounded by the merchants' use of strange vineyard names, talk of tannin and acid levels and obscure vineyard conditions of different years. Conversely, most of the other off-trade shops were filled by people with no interest in wine, a dismal range, and no skills or inclination to sell it. The consumer was consistently discouraged from buying wine on a regular basis – a very different story today.

The new face of wine retailing

While this is principally a book on wines in restaurants, it is worth briefly considering the revitalization of the off-trade in recent years for the major effect it has had on the wine-buying public. For the consumer the most visible changes are the huge development in the range of products carried by the big chains of shops, and more recently the advent of multiple branding strategies. Out have gone the know-nothing-about-wine shop managers described above, and in have come often younger, better qualified managers who are keen to sell wines alongside their ranges of beers and spirits. Rather than having only one style of shop, a variety of outlets have developed ranging from plain off-licences, where the emphasis remains on 'traditional' off-licence goods such as beer, cigarettes and spirits, through to wine specialists and wine warehouses.

Perhaps the most interesting of these subbrands within the large off-licence companies are those targeting the middle-class or wine-based sector of the market. In the UK these include 'Oddbins', Thresher's 'Wine Rack' chain, 'Victoria Wine Cellars' and Greenall's 'Wine Cellar'. Often managed by those who are particularly keen on wine, these stores are designed and decorated to look like traditional wine merchants, using claret cases, wooden shelving and false ceilings to give a feel reminiscent of cellars or French caves (Fattorini, 1994b: 9). But while they aim to give the appearance of being a traditional wine merchant in many cases they attract a very different and in some ways a new sort of customer.

From any standpoint the UK is a far more middle-class country than it was in the aftermath of World War II. By this we mean that more people own their own homes, have cars and take foreign holidays, not that they necessarily consider themselves middle class. (If anything people increasingly claim to be working class, Jacobs and Worcester, 1990: 134–44). Together with such symbols of middle-class status comes wine, which is always perceived as a middle-class drink in Britain. Therefore it is no surprise that the nation's consumption of wine has increased so dramatically in the years since the war, not least in the Thatcher years of the 1980s when government policy broadened Britain's middle class and sales of wine increased at a phenomenal rate. To satisfy the demand from these customers a new style of wine retailing was needed. Traditional wine merchants were seen as too stuffy; their vast ranges and besuited, well-spoken staff were intimidating to those unused to that sort of shop. Off-licences, although familiar, carried a limited range. To fill the void came bigger wine selections on supermarket shelves, making wine just a regular weekly purchase, and specialist brands within wine retail groups that aimed to fill the gap between the traditional wine merchant and the 'beer and fags' shop.

The wine specialist brands of the large drinks retailers have a very broad range of wines, often to the extent of slightly reducing the range of spirits and beers to premium brands and specialist or foreign products. The fittings give them the feel of a wine shop, as mentioned above, but they are also very obviously branded, retaining an overall similarity. Customers have the security of familiar surroundings and, most importantly, nobody needs to be a wine expert to shop there. The most intimidating aspect for many wine shoppers appears to be that there is a huge array of names about which they know nothing.

- What do they taste like?
- Will it go with the food they have chosen?
- Where does it come from?

Although the staff in the traditional store would be happy to help, many customers prefer not to have to ask.

Wine carries with it great social currency. To be an expert on wines has long been regarded as essential for the true gentleman and asking the sales assistant for help is almost an admission of coarseness. Thorstein Veblen (1899: 44), in his illuminating treatment of turn-of-the-century leisured Americans, writes, 'In the nature of things, luxuries and the comforts of life belong to the leisure class... Certain victuals, and more particularly certain beverages, are strictly reserved for the use of the superior class.' While in today's more egalitarian society this sort of viewpoint is ignored, and rightly so, there appears to be a lingering belief that lack of knowledge about wine is not something you want to advertise. To get around this problem and limit the possibility of social exchange and embarrassment, the wine-based brands of the big drinks firms use point-of-sale (POS) material. These range from little descriptive cards with each wine, describing its style, origin and price, to much larger cards or neck collars on specific wines that are being promoted, particularly own label lines. Shoppers can browse in these shops with only a limited wine knowledge ('I like red/white that is sweet/dry') without needing a sales assistant in attendance.

Restaurants and the wine revolution

While some of the most visible changes in wine sales have happened in high street retailing, the credit for this transformation goes to restaurants. As Christopher Driver points out in *The British at Table* (1983: 112), changes in what people drink appear to come more easily than changes in what people eat: 'It may feel easier as well as cheaper to order a strange drink in a pub – or to sip someone else's – than it is to ask for mouthfuls from someone else's plate.' Certainly those who have studied the sociology of food and drink invariably report that offering food to acquaintances is always taken more seriously and is a more intimate act than offering somebody a drink (Douglas and Nicod, 1974). As there is a sense of added intimacy in the offer of a meal, people tend to play safe and go for a choice they know will be enjoyed. Drinks, on the other hand, carry a greatly reduced status as indicators of friendship and so can be experimented with rather more. When people did begin to experiment with food and drink after the austerity of World War II it was therefore understandable that the first (and most obvious) change would appear in what they drank.

As far as wine is concerned, any major change in consumption patterns is going to start in the restaurant. Even today a great many people do not drink alcohol on a regular basis. Only 58% of adults drink alcohol (in whatever form) at least monthly, with those drinking most frequently tending to be men, the young and those in socio-economic groups A and B (*The Drink Pocket Book*, 1994: 24).

Yet while many may drink very little in the home, they do drink when there is a special occasion or when dining out. The importance of this occasional consumption of wine is particularly strong in restaurants where the appeal lies not in any one particular aspect of the meal, the food, the atmosphere or the wines but in the experience of the whole, or, as it has been put, in the 'meal experience'. When eating out in restaurants few people are unaware of the order of drinks in the meal. This order begins with an aperitif, either in a bar area or at the table, followed by wine during the meal and occasionally a digestif like a brandy or liqueur to finish off. People invariably order a drink with which they are very familiar for their aperitif (beer, gin and tonic, sherry). If they need help from a sommelier it is with choosing a wine – when faced with pages of unfamiliar names they may be less confident. Yet despite many people drinking very little wine at home, convention and experience teaches them that to leave out wine in a restaurant would be to lose a part of that 'meal experience' (Campbell-Smith, 1967).

As eating out in restaurants has become an increasingly common experience, with part of that experience being the enjoyment of wine, drinking wine has inevitably become more customary. Added to this, wine is by far the easiest component of the restaurant experience to transfer into the home (as opposed to the restaurant cooking or waiting staff). As wine has become more readily available in the high street and supermarkets it has begun to appear at dinner parties and family meals.

The question of mark-ups

When people have reached the stage where they are buying wine in restaurants or for themselves at home, they begin to question the levels of mark-up that they see on restaurant winelists. Many large hotels, which were the precursors to modern restaurants with the best chefs and food, would traditionally buy their wine direct from producers or brokers, ship it to their cellars and store it themselves. To cover the costs of this exercise (not to mention making up for having so much capital tied up in stock) they would mark up wines at around 200% on cost. For most consumers there was little problem in this as they had nothing to compare it to, with wine merchants catering only to a very specialist market. Again, change came after World War II when restaurants (increasingly run by chef/proprietors without massive cash reserves to build up cellars) began to buy their wine from wholesale wine merchants. These merchants would deliver small amounts on credit terms which gave shrewd restaurateurs the chance to sell the wine before they had paid for it. Restaurateurs were then in a position to reduce their mark-ups, which has to some extent happened. Change though has been painfully slow and has left restaurateurs with a reputation for excessive profit-taking on wines. In the 1950s only a few 'famously brazen restaurateurs in Britain, most of them French' (Driver, 1983: 114) kept their mark-ups at the immediate post-war (200%) level. Most approached the levels most commonly seen now of around 120%, giving a restaurant a return of around 60% on the final retail price.

For the restaurateur this profit goes some way towards making up for the low cash margins available on food sales. To the customers, who are increasingly aware of the retail cost of wine, it often seems as if they are paying at least as much again for somebody to open and pour the bottle. This price consciousness exists not only because of the proliferation of high street wine retailers and their broader ranges, but also because customers are far more likely to have travelled abroad to countries where wine drinking is a regular part of daily life and duty levels are much lower, revealing the true cost of the wine at its source. This has given customers a far greater awareness of wine costs generally, removing much of the opportunity for capitalizing on the luxury value of wine, an unavoidable consequence of the change in wine's status from occasional indulgence to everyday commodity. Customer awareness of the true cost of wine has also increased through the relaxation of border controls, particularly with France, making them far more informed of the various components of the cost of wine and thus the likely margins being made by the restaurateur. Unfortunately, since wine is so much part of the meal experience, with many feeling obliged to buy wine when eating in a restaurant, the knowledge of what that wine could be bought for in the high street or in France can all too easily lead to feelings of resentment being directed at the restaurateur. Customers can feel bound by manners to pay what they regard as a ridiculous price for wine. At this point the importance of good staff training comes into play, in order to take the customers' attention away from the cost of everything and to make sure that they feel they have received good value for money.

THE NEED FOR MORE HIGHLY TRAINED STAFF

Curiously, despite food and wine living in such a natural partnership, apart from the odd chapter in gastronomy textbooks and little 'I recommend' footnotes in some recipe books, the two are treated as totally different and separate. The humorous *The Official Foodie Handbook* (Barr and Levy, 1984) claims in a chapter entitled 'Wine has its place (second)': 'in your heart, you must be a Foodie or a Grapie [a wine lover]. Foodies know instinctively that it is dangerous to food to really like wine'; and later 'Food is noble. Drink goes with it.' This opposition between the two partners at the heart of the 'meal experience' is further emphasised by the way in which they are treated in many catering and cookery courses. While the main component of courses is taken up with food preparation, menu design or similar food-based modules, wine is relegated to a separate class or given a series of lectures/demonstrations on its own.

This is at odds with the situation in Italy, for example, where the two are often integrated together. As opposed to specific food or wine tasting, different wines and foods are tried together, highlighting those foods that are natural partners, as well as those with little affinity for each other. Sommeliers then have a thorough grounding not only in wines, particularly in terms of how they taste, but can also assess how they will interact with foods. This appears to come from a far more holistic view of the meal experience in many Mediterranean countries.

The division between the two worlds of food and wine is also evident in the position of the sommelier or wine waiter. Wine waiters carry with them many of the characteristics associated with the high street wine merchant. They are always believed to be (and good ones invariably are) experts on wine. Problems in how they are perceived by the public appear to come from the way they interact with their customers in the course of advising them, serving them and occasionally dealing with their complaints. For the most part these interactions take place with the sommeliers in something of a dominant position by virtue of their knowledge of wine. Some take advantage of their wine knowledge, like Luigi, head wine waiter at the Piccadilly Ritz Hotel: 'he sells what he wants and not what the customer wants. His example of this power is when a customer has ordered a wine but, on tasting, does not like it. Luigi replaces it with the same offending wine' (Finkelstein, 1989: 57). When the public inevitably find out about this sort of practice, they see themselves as being hoodwinked and the next time a sommelier says 'Excellent choice, sir' (with some justification it is felt that sommeliers assume men in mixed parties will choose), the diners wonder to what extent they are being laughed at. The customers come to fear choosing a wine, wondering whether they will make the 'right' choice, despite it being impossible for them to tell anyway.

Fortunately there are many very fine sommeliers and their numbers are increasing. Emily Green (1995) describes how Sylvano Giraldin, manager of Albert Roux's Le Gavroche in Mayfair, London, 'will be for ever a hero for a particularly gentle bit of instruction. During my first visit, we ordered a Volnay. "And would you like that ever so slightly chilled?" he asked, in a voice that subtly told me that this was just the thing to request.' The fact that good wine service is apparently so rare that it merits comment in a newspaper highlights the importance of good staff training. As wine becomes far more a part of daily life this training needs to consist of more than isolated modules on courses or one or two wine tastings on a gastronomy course.

The knowledgeable customer

Food and drink are very fashionable; great social currency is put on being capable of cooking a superb dinner party, or knowing just which restaurants are 'in' at the moment, or even better having long patronized those which have just been discovered by everyone else. It is no accident that *The Official Foodie*

Handbook (Barr and Levy, 1984) was published in association with the society monthly *Harpers and Queen*. The book describes 'foodieism' as an 'upwardly mobile activity'. The broadening of the British middle class has made 'foodieism' available or affordable to far more people and this is evident in its increasing prominence in the media. There are specialist magazines devoted to food and drink (although interestingly these invariably concentrate on either food or drink, unlike the Italian *L'Etichetta* and the French *Cuisine et Vins de France*, and the monthly *Gault-Millau* which take a continental, holistic view of the meal). All national broadsheet newspapers and many tabloids have a regular food and drink column. On television and radio there are programmes such as 'Food and Drink', 'The Food Programme', even food quiz shows such as BBC Radio Four's 'Questions of Taste'. Television comedy and drama also feature food, with both the series' 'Chef' and 'Pie in the Sky' proving popular (Fattorini, 1994a: 24–8). These programmes are undoubtedly developed to serve a wider interest held by the public in food and drink and the industries that supply it.

For some though, particularly those characterized by the foodie or grapie labels, this interest goes much further. Increasingly they are enrolling on cookery and wine courses, some of which were previously reserved for trade only – for example, the Wine and Spirit Educational Trust (WSET) courses which lead to its Certificate, Higher Certificate and Diploma. Although described as 'austere' and 'factual and didactic' (Grigg, 1995: 29), the courses are favoured by those who wish to learn about wine precisely because they are used by the trade (both in restaurants and off-licences), and because they are not based exclusively in London. While the importance for staff to have these qualifications is developed later on, the fact that customers may also have them makes the issue increasingly important.

Staff training: the old school

Perhaps because of the traditional nature of the jobs within them and the sense of importance attached to historical pedigree, selling wine in both the off and on trade has had its traditional route of entry. In the off-trade, particularly wine merchants, the time-honoured means of entry was to learn how wine was made on site. After school and possibly university, young men (rarely women) would go usually to France and work in the cellars and vineyards of a producer, often in one of the more prestigious wine-growing regions such as Bordeaux or Burgundy. After that he would return to Britain as a proficient French speaker with a good working knowledge of wines to join a reputable firm and settle into importing and selling. If this appears to be a rather ad hoc system for joining an industry involved in the trade of vast quantities of wine, it is perhaps because entry to the trade has always been so. There are no specialist university or college courses for budding wine merchants, and many come into the trade after having trained in an altogether different discipline. The law, in particular, seems to provide many raw recruits for the wine trade, and Michael Broadbent, head of Christie's Wine Department and arguably Britain's most respected and experienced merchant, trained initially as an architect.

Within the on-trade too, those who set out to make wine their career appear to have enjoyed training by the luck of where they were and the enthusiasm of their superiors. Some tales appear to have been romanticized, but the initial start as the cellar boy taken under the wing of an old master or time spent abroad all add to the mystique of the job, particularly to the customer, even if they are of little use to a pragmatic and ambitious young school leaver.

A new sense of professionalism

Specialist in-house wine and spirit training programmes have developed in large hotel and restaurant groups, rather like those of large off-licence chains. Resources in these companies allow for specialist training staff to develop and implement a variety of training programmes (in large hotel groups there may be a person per outlet). As far as wines are concerned these have often followed the format of the WSET examinations, so much so that they are 'developed in conjunction with' the WSET or are accepted as an equivalent qualification, allowing the candidate to go forward to the next level within the Trust.

For smaller outlets, examinations are usually taken entirely within the format of the WSET. The exact content of each examination is developed in Chapter 8, but briefly the Certificate develops basic knowledge of wine production areas and methods. The major regions seen in restaurant wine lists are covered and there are descriptions of styles. The Higher Certificate goes into more detail, covering the annual cycle of vineyard work and the regions of the world in which wine is made. The final examination is the Diploma, a challenging two-year course covering the wine-producing regions of the world comprehensively. The course includes practical details about wine importing regulations and procedure, viticulture and vinification and wine technology, as well as two in-depth modules on whisky and brandy.

Described in the prospectus as a course aimed at those in 'a managerial position or [who] may be under consideration for promotion to such a position', the course is as far as many take their wine education. For those who wish to go further (and are deemed capable) the diploma is the basic entry level qualification for the very demanding entrance examinations to the Institute of Masters of Wine, leading to the qualification Master of Wine (MW). So demanding is this course that those who have passed it since its establishment in 1953 number little over 200, although the numbers taking (and passing) the examinations (six in three days, three written, three tasting) are growing slowly.

WINE AND RESTAURANTS IN THE FUTURE

Complacency in all those who sell wine has never been quite so out of place as at the present time. Even over the last ten years the changes in producing nations and consumption patterns have been immense. In Driver's (1983) study of Britain's post-war dining habits, he noted how Britain had increased its wine consumption by some 250%.

> **NEW ZEALAND**
>
> Although far more reliant on sheep and dairy farming than wine, New Zealand's relatively small and recent output of wine has won international acclaim. In fact New Zealand's winemakers have often been credited with using the infrastructure of the domestic dairy industry to help them produce wines. Stainless steel equipment like that used in milk production is easy to clean, inert and provides very little opportunity for oxygen to spoil wine. All these factors are essential for producing clean, crisp whites for drinking young — something that New Zealand has proved most adept at. Although wines from New Zealand are not the cheapest in the world, they have made a big impact in the middle ground of wines between £5.00 and £10.00, wines which frequently feature on restaurant wine lists.
>
> Most famous for its Sauvignon Blanc wines, the country actually has far higher plantings of Chardonnay and the once predominant Muller-Thurgau. It also produces a certain amount of Cabernet Sauvignon and Pinot Noir, with some commentators speculating that it may prove an ideal home for this last, hard to cultivate variety. Recently some critics of New Zealand wines have suggested that their immense popularity, particularly in Britain, owes a great deal to hyping by wine journalists keen to be rewarded with trips to the country by grateful producers. Given the uncertainty about the influence of journalists over consumer wine choice, this is hard to substantiate or disprove.

New producer nations and fashions

Had the amazing increases in wine consumption simply been in wines from Britain's traditional suppliers, then life for restaurants would indeed have been easy. However, much of the increased consumption has been in wines from new wine-producing countries with former bulk producers moving into quality wine. For those who are to sell wine this has meant changes in training to much broader syllabuses which encompass countries that after the war hardly produced any wine of note, if any wine at all. Many of these countries have come to the fore with remarkable speed, not least in the quality wine market which is what matters most to restaurateurs. A good intrinsic product that is accurately tailored to appeal to a broad market, coupled with good professional public relations, can establish a new individual producer and even a new country in a very short time.

Examples of countries which have become established recently are New Zealand, Chile and many former communist states in Eastern Europe. All these countries produce wines that have a strong appeal with the British public, especially the middle market. Much of the success of these products is based on the fact that they have become very fashionable. Perhaps the most impressive example of this has been the New Zealand wine producer Cloudy Bay. Based in Marlborough on New Zealand's South Island, Cloudy Bay's vineyards

CHILE

Although often heralded as being part of a New Wave of producer nations, Chile was in fact first planted with vines in the sixteenth century. Today it is noted for production of varietal wines, i.e. those produced from a single grape variety and described on the label as such (as opposed to being named after a region). Red varieties such as Cabernet Sauvignon and Merlot and whites like Chardonnay and Sauvignon Blanc are particularly common.

Perhaps the most remarkable feature of Chile's wine-producing industry is its freedom from Phylloxera, an aphid whose arrival in Europe in the late nineteenth century almost heralded the end of the wine industry in some parts. Yellow and with a complex life cycle, phylloxera (although more properly *Daktulosphaira vitifoliae*) feeds on the sap of vines while living on its roots. Wild vines in North America where phylloxera originated were able to heal the wounds caused by the louse, preventing infection and stemming the flow of sap. European domesticated vines used for wine production had no such resistance to infestation and soon succumbed. In Chile the combined effects of the Pacific Ocean, the Andes and strict quarantine have meant that phylloxera is unknown. Thus while European winemakers must endure the added cost of grafting their vines onto phylloxera-resistant rootstock and spraying them, Chileans can grow vines without fear of infestation.

produce a number of different wines, a red Cabernet/Merlot blend, a sparkling wine called 'Pelorus', a sweet late harvest Riesling and two whites, Chardonnay and its flagship wine, Sauvignon Blanc. This wine is such a cult that it sells out within hours of reaching many retailers, who receive not what they would like to order, but rather what Cloudy Bay's distributors allocate to their store. What is most important in the success of Cloudy Bay is not so much the quality of the wine, although it is very good and arguably one of New Zealand's best, but that it has created such a fashionable wine. For the restaurateur this is very important. Restaurants also find that success and failure are reliant on whether they are perceived as fashionable. As interest in wine becomes ever more widespread among the British public, it should be expected that customers will begin to notice very fashionable wines on wine lists. Restaurateurs who keep a standard list of old favourites from traditional, wine-producing countries may very quickly find that they are left with out-of-date lists that give their restaurants a dated image.

Alternatively we may find in the future that demand will shift towards providing better value table wines. On the continent many restaurant customers (who eat out more frequently than their British counterparts) are not concerned with drinking fine wines from famous regions every time they dine. This is partly because the frequency makes the meal less of an occasion and so there is not the desire to treat (or impress) their companions. In Britain the customers eat out less frequently and the occasion is still seen by many as a special treat and worth going to the extra fuss (and extra expense) of choosing a special wine. Were the situation in Britain to change and people were to start eating out far more frequently as a matter of course, then it could well be the case that the frequent diners would demand better quality table wines, reserving quality wines for special occasions.

Future changes within restaurants

In relation to its importance, the attention given to wine by restaurants is often minimal. The expense of storing and serving wine is small, particularly when restaurateurs have made full use of the credit facilities and delivery services offered by most decent wholesale wine merchants. In their desire to gain business many merchants do not stop there but offer free winelist printing services and help for restaurateurs in best merchandising their wines. Yet with all this support restaurants are still able to get away with marking up their wines (on cost) at between 100% and 200%. Even when a restaurateur devotes one member of staff full time to selling wine (and even then it is rare to find a 'sommelier' who does not double up on waitering to some extent) wine still remains a remarkably profitable part of the restaurant's operation.

Why quite so many restaurateurs treat their wine lists with relative indifference is therefore difficult to assess. A merchant selling to hotels and restaurants is likely to hear comments such as 'do whatever you want, just don't fiddle around with it to much' when trying to change a hopelessly out-of-date wine list. Food may be what makes or breaks a restaurant in the public's eye and in the pages of guidebooks, but indifference like this to such an important earner in a restaurant is what makes many successful restaurants fail. Managers and owners must become far more aware of the importance of wine as a cash earner in their restaurants if they are to use it to best effect and avoid becoming one of the thousands of restaurants that fail every year.

This situation may well worsen in years to come if, as pointed out above, diners become more aware of restaurant mark-up levels and there is pressure to reduce them. Currently it is the case that the huge profits made by wine mean that drinkers effectively subsidize non-drinkers. Food sales may pay for themselves, but may provide such a small cash margin (if a very large percentage margin) that many of the overheads are paid for out of wine sales.

Restaurateurs must become wine experts

During the research for this book a restaurateur admitted that when he opened his own restaurant his knowledge of wine was minimal. He had to learn about wine by trial and error, discovering from his mistakes and recovering from them with hard work and a bit of luck. The restaurant is now phenomenally successful, winning accolades from the guides and praise from customers, not least for a superb and innovative wine list and a fantastic range of wines by the glass. Yet this was no newcomer to the restaurant business; he had trained at a top catering college and gained years of experience in hotel management.

If career caterers like this find it hard to deal with wines, those hundreds who come into the restaurant business every year from other backgrounds are going to find it doubly difficult.

If restaurateurs want to avoid going bankrupt they will have to take a far greater personal control over their wine lists. The future may well see great pressure on them to reduce mark-ups on wine. This will have the twofold effect of forcing food sales to pay their way rather more than is customary, and making selection of wines for their ability to earn money absolutely vital. For many restaurateurs the development of a wine list is 'one of the perks of the job', involving free tastings, lunches from merchants and afternoons quietly discussing which grape varieties to feature most strongly. Alternatively it is a job left to specialist wine staff whose training leads them to choose wines on the basis of what they feel fits in best, rather than necessarily what provides the best return.

The need for financial realism by restaurateurs will also mean that they must provide lists that keep up with the latest trends in wine drinking. It is no longer acceptable to have a list that simply provides one or two wines from the major French and German regions along with a few old Italian favourites and an Australian or two for good measure. To be truly successful, wine lists must keep up with the latest producing regions and with wines that are currently fashionable on the high street.

The need to keep wine lists up to date with new regions (and increasingly grape varieties and production methods) need not be incompatible with the need for a new sense of financial realism in wine selection for lists. Invariably new regions provide very good value, but they can come in and out of favour relatively quickly. The producers in new regions can also become far less competitive as they become established. This means that to have a successful and profitable list requires a proactive approach from the restaurateur, keeping an eye on what is happening in the wine world, who is competitive (remembering exchange rates can make a wine overpriced as much as producers' price increases), and what wines customers are prepared to pay a premium for.

Internally too, restaurateurs must take a greater interest and control. Having had experience of the way some restaurateurs deal with their wine lists, it does not come as a surprise when otherwise popular and successful restaurants go bankrupt. Many owners have little real sense of how much money each bottle is making, which are their most profitable wines and how much they contribute to the financial success of the restaurant. Keith Floyd in his autobiography (1988) tells how simple accounting errors led him seriously into debt. Despite running several restaurants very successfully he made a simple error in accounting for VAT on wines. As he puts it:

> In my philanthropic attempts to dispense goodwill and, above all, good wines to all men I had developed a non-rip-off system for people who chose really expensive wine. Wine that cost me up to five pounds to buy, I marked up by sixty per cent, but wines that cost more than ten pounds and in some cases fifteen to twenty per bottle, I merely stuck three pounds

on per bottle. Thus I made, or so I thought, about the same amount – roughly three quid a bottle – from everything I sold. Result: the customer would appreciate this and drink more wine. But in reality a bottle of wine which cost me fifteen pounds and fifteen per cent VAT, which I'd overlooked, and I sold for eighteen pounds, including VAT, was only making about thirty pence, minus the ten per cent interest the wine company charged me for being a late payer bought the profit down to about zero.

(Floyd, 1988: 68–9)

Errors like this are compounded by financial myths and half truths in the industry that seem to become ingrained at the expense of common sense. A classic example is the treatment of sparkling wine mark-ups. Although few restaurants are keen to advertise their mark-up levels, running down the lists most wines show similar levels of percentage mark-up until the Champagnes and sparkling wines. This is because many restaurateurs feel they will not sell it if it is marked up to provide the standard 60% profit, as it is usually one of the most expensive wines on the list, with any Champagne rarely selling for less than £10.00 a bottle. Even so, still wine that is comparable in price with Champagne is marked up like the rest of the list to return 60% on retail. This policy is despite Champagne and sparkling wines being bought as a celebration drink when price is less of an issue for the customer than having something fizzy. Furthermore, oversupply of Champagne in recent years has led to a profusion of Premier Prix brands, which (given careful selection) have a low price that makes them ideal as house Champagnes with very healthy mark-ups. Unfortunately, force of habit on the part of many restaurateurs has led them to ignore what could be highly profitable, in favour of losing still wine sales through excessive marking up and profit on Champagne sales.

SUMMARY

Although the British wine trade has had a long and distinguished history, it has had to work hard to keep up with the changes of the last fifty years. Not only has the market for wine grown immeasurably, but a new type of consumer has developed who is far removed from the leisured, moneyed wine drinkers of Britain's past. However, the trade was well established to deal with these changes and has coped admirably. Wine retailing has changed beyond recognition in recent years and restaurants must now continue in that trend. Modern consumers appear more knowledgeable than ever before, but also more relaxed about wine drinking as it becomes increasingly an everyday activity. The next chapter will now look in greater detail at the changes in the modern wine consumers and try to build up a profile of what they are like and how we as wine sellers can satisfy them.

QUESTIONS AND EXERCISES

1. Go to a number of different wine merchants and look at how they market themselves to their customers. Are they targeting a specific

type of wine customer or are they going for the whole market? What tools do they use to promote themselves to their favoured market group?
2. Start a 'Service Diary'. Visit wine merchants or buy wine in a restaurant or bar and examine how you are treated. Does whoever serves you proffer advice or must you ask for it? Do they assume a level of knowledge or do they describe the most basic of wine facts. Afterwards note down what you find and compare it with service encounters in other environments—buying clothes or drinks in a pub, for instance.
3. Try to find out more about the history of the wine trade — perhaps beginning with Henry of Anjou's marriage to Eleanor of Aquitaine or the Methuen Treaty. You will find that some of the things you learn will help to give 'personality' to the wine you sell (see Chapter 7).
4. 'The wine trade is a gentleman's profession' — is this remark, true or relevant and has it ever been?
5. 'Wine expertise is not important to sell the stuff, just a love of what it tastes like'—discuss.

FURTHER READING

There is a number of good books on the development of the world and UK wine trade. Some of these are also mentioned at the end of Chapter 4. Specific books on the wine trade include *Anatomy of the Wine Trade* by Simon Loftus (1985) and *Wine and the Vine* by Tim Unwin (1991) – 'a historical geography of viticulture (grapevine growing) and the wine trade'. Two books by Andrew Barr, *Wine Snobbery* (1988) and *Drink* (1995) also provide fascinating insights into the growth and development of the wine business.

For those who want to keep up to date with thinking in the wine business, the trade journals *Harpers* and *Wine and Spirit International* give trade news and developments, while the more academic *International Journal of Wine Marketing* publishes articles on a range of subjects concerning wine sales and marketing. The journal is published by MCB University Press and edited by Michael Howley of the University of Surrey.

2 The modern wine consumer

> ***Key concepts***
>
> The main concepts covered in this chapter are:
> - who drinks what;
> - new consumer attitudes towards wine;
> - what's in a name?

INTRODUCTION

While writing this book I visited a restaurant (with a particularly good wine list) where there was a set of cartoons on the wall. Each was meant to represent a different sort of wine with the caricature of a person. For instance, there was a portly, rumbustuous looking gentleman with a red face and tweed suit with the caption 'a sturdy, full-bodied wine, packed with flavour'. Alternatively there was a picture of an oily biker, with the slogan 'a rather coarse wine'. Among other things these cartoons highlighted the characters that many people apply to wine as well as the personalities whom they expect to drink them: the well-dressed, middle-class cartoon characters were wines from classic regions of Europe, the fashionable and nouveau riche were from the New World producer nations; the scruffy ones were table wines.

Now for most people the importance of such characterizations probably goes no further than being mildly entertained by these cartoons. But for restaurateurs the implications run deeper, particularly if they are trying to create a 'wine experience' for customers in their restaurant. If it is true that a certain customer 'type' tends to drink red wines from the classic French regions of Bordeaux, Burgundy or the Rhône, then it becomes very important be able to identify that 'type' when they visit the restaurant. Alternatively, if a restaurant attracts a large number of young professionals, how can it find out (other than by trial and error) what wines this group particularly likes and those for which it would be prepared to pay a premium.

The purpose of this chapter is therefore to look at modern wine drinking habits and to develop some sort of framework of consumer attitudes both to wine consumption in general as well as specific wine types. The first part of the chapter, 'Who drinks what', draws largely on statistical information, observing changes in UK drinking habits over the past ten or so years. The second part, 'New consumer attitudes towards wine', considers some of the values that consumers give to wine in general and to specific wines. Many of these attitudes appear to be based on spurious, illogical and (most frequently) intangible factors. Yet for those who wish to create a 'wine experience' for their customers, understanding which wines appear to appeal to which customers can be a key to maximizing sales and revenue.

WHO DRINKS WHAT?

Many writers in both books and periodicals have described the massive changes in drinking habits over the last twenty to forty years, in particular the increase in wine consumption. These statements are often backed up by specific figures. However, it is worth investigating this increased wine consumption in rather more detail.

How much do we drink?

As a nation we are gradually spending more on drink in general and wine in particular. At current (1996) prices we went from a total expenditure on 'drink products' including soft drinks of £31,907,000,000 in 1970 to £428,084,000,000 in the most recently available year for statistics, 1994 – an increase of over 1300%. The increase in expenditure on wine consumption over the same period was from a sum of £297,000,000 (again at current prices) in 1970 to £4,998,000,000 in 1994, an even more impressive increase of over 1800% (see Figure 2.1).

However, these statistics are hard to understand in any meaningful way as they do not take into account changes in the nation's population over that extensive period. Equally they do not record changes in the type of wine consumed. These differences can be seen by examining statistics that measure our per capita consumption of pure (100%) alcohol in the various alcoholic drinks taken. The UK's total per capita consumption of pure alcohol remains relatively consistent. In the period 1975 to 1994 the amount measured in litres per annum (LPA) varied between a high of 10.00 LPA and a low of 8.93 LPA, but with no discernible trend emerging. These two figures in fact appeared within three years of each other, the first occurring in 1979, the second in 1982. Figures for other years invariably lie between these two, with no significant trend up or down over the period (HM Customs and Excise, Office of Population Censuses and Surveys).

The UK consumption of wine over the period 1975–94 is much more interesting (see Figure 2.2). In 1975 0.88 LPA of pure alcohol was consumed per year in the form of wine made from fresh grapes. Of this the largest component was 'Still Light' wine at 0.52 LPA. Over the next twenty years

22 | The modern wine consumer

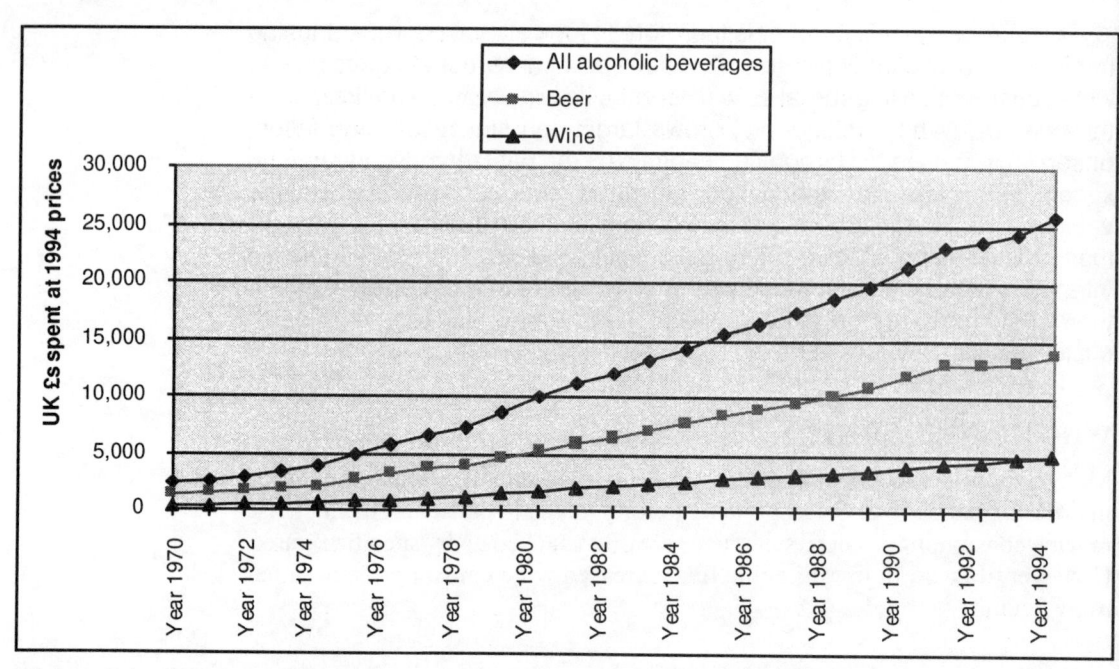

Figure 2.1 UK expenditure on alcoholic beverages, 1975–94.
Source: Central Statistical Office; *The Drink Pocket Book* (1996: 19).

DEFINITIONS OF 'WINE'

Often in statistical information, the information about wine is broken up into a variety of categories. The main distinction is between 'Wine of Fresh Grape' and 'Made Wine'. 'Wine of Fresh Grape' constitutes the majority of wines imported and sold in Britain and is what most people understand by wine – that is grapes picked and fermented, without major adjustment, in the region of origin. This includes still table wines, sparkling wines and fortified wines, although these subdivisions are often given in tables of consumption statistics.

'Made Wine' is the term applied to wine made from grape concentrate rather than fresh grape juice. For people in the UK perhaps the most readily available form of grape concentrate is that used in home wine-making kits. For many producers making wine with grape concentrate means that they can produce all year round (it is far more economical to store for later use and can be transported elsewhere for later production). In the UK the most important form of 'Made Wine' has long been 'British Wine'. This is not to be confused with 'English Wine' which is made from grapes grown and fermented in the UK. British wine is made with imported concentrate, often shipped from Cyprus. Probably the most common form of this was British and Cyprus 'Sherry', a term allowed until recently through an exemption in European Law.

though the change has been dramatic. By 1994 per capita consumption in terms of pure alcohol consumed had increased by over 300% to 1.60 LPA. Obviously if this had been done in a period when total alcohol consumption by the nation had remained relatively consistent, there must have been losers to make up for the strides forward being made by still wine. Certainly beer suffered over that period going from 5.84 LPA to 4.83 LPA. The percentage drop of around 17% does not do justice to the volume drop of around one litre of pure alcohol consumed in that form per head over the 19 years. Interestingly while by 1994 the nation was drinking one litre per head of pure alcohol less in the form of beer than it had in 1975, it was consuming just over a litre (1.08L) more per head each year in the form of still light wine.

The UK population appears to be drinking about the same amount of alcohol as 20 years ago, but is now consuming more of it as wine and less as beer. For the restaurant trade though another interesting indicator of drink expenditure is what sort of proportion of personal expenditure it comprises and whether the purse strings of UK wine consumers are being loosened or tightened with regard to wine. Over a slightly longer period (1970 to 1994) they appear to be loosening, but seem very sensitive to prevailing economic conditions (see Figure 2.3). In 1970 0.85% of UK personal expenditure went on wines (all types) whereas by 1994 this had risen to 1.05%. Although this rise may not

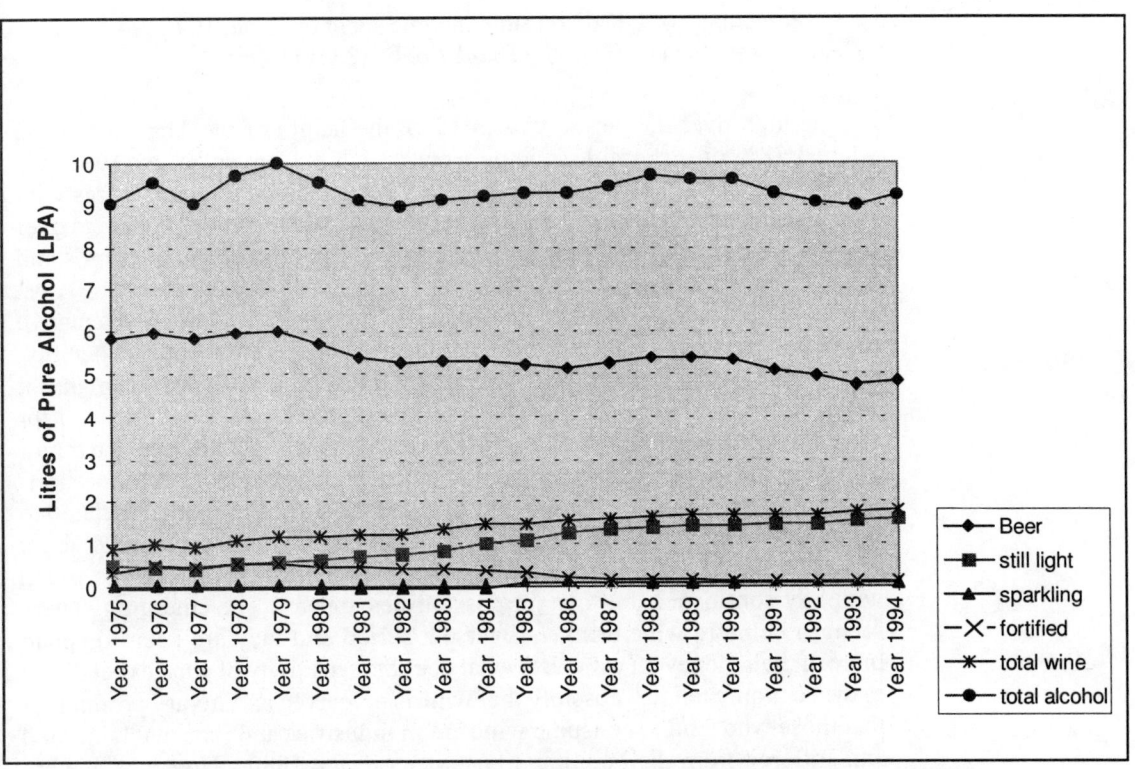

Figure 2.2 UK per capita consumption at 100% alcohol by beverage type, 1975–94. Source: HM Customs and Excise, OPCS; *The Drink Pocket Book* (1996:17).

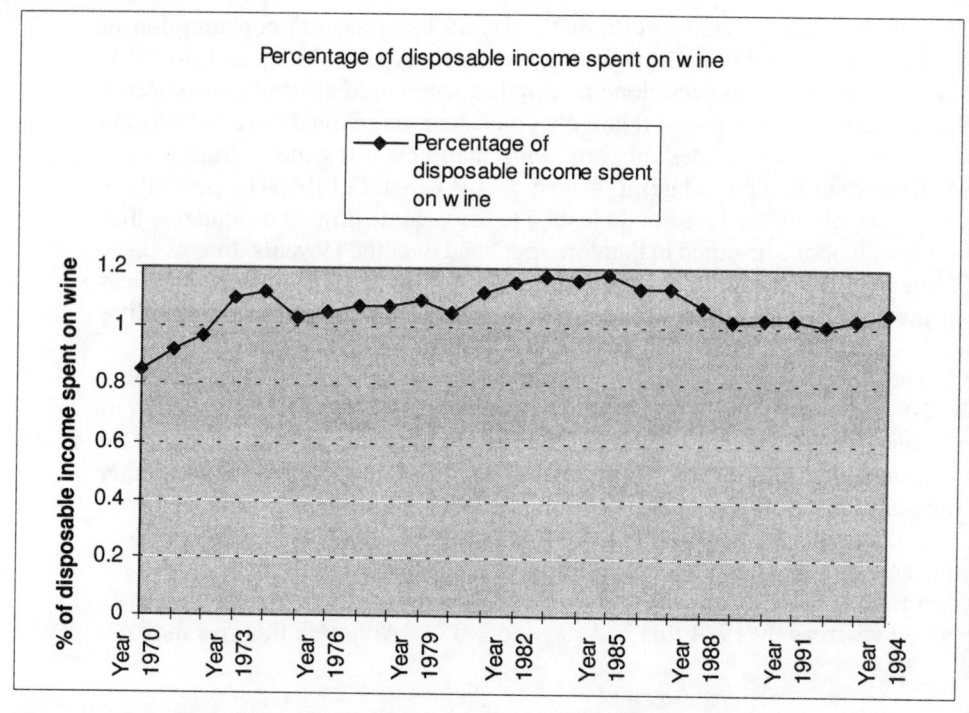

Figure 2.3 Percentage of UK disposable income spent on wine, 1970–94.
Source: Central Statistical Office; *The Drink Pocket Book* (1996: 22).

is. The high over the period was in 1985, the height of the Thatcher years, when 1.18% of disposable income went on wine. Conversely by 1992, the depths of recession, this had slumped to 1.01%. Compare these figures with beer which showed a steady decline in its claim on the nation's pockets over the same period with only marginal changes during the economic highs and lows of the two decades.

One should be wary of reading too much into these figures but a few tentative suggestions could be allowed. First, while wine consumption appears healthy, it is fair to say that its sensitivity to the economic health of the nation makes it a riskier proposition in the short term (all the statistics seem to bode well for the long term economic viability of wine). Conversely, while beer, the major player in the alcoholic beverages market, is relatively insensitive to short-term economic change, over the long term it is in a decline, perhaps related to various environmental factors. Second, what comments can be made about wine consumers from these figures? The answer is probably not too much with any confidence, but certain possibilities appear to be emerging. There seem to be more wine drinkers over the period and they are keen to spend more of their money on wine. But what does the sensitivity of wine expenditure to the economy tell us? Possibly that wine is perceived as a luxury product, or that those who tend to consume wine are in industries and jobs that benefited and suffered from the boom and bust years of the 1980s. However, we are now getting out of the realms of how much wine we drink and rather more luxury product, or that those who tend to consume wine are in industries and jobs that benefited and suffered from the boom and bust years of the 1980s. However, we are now getting out of the realms of how much wine we drink and rather more into the subject of who drinks wine.

Who drinks wine?

The idea that wine is a luxury product with its consumption concentrated among the middle classes is in fact backed up by other data. In socio-economic groups AB, 48% claimed they had drunk wine in the last week, as opposed to only 23% of C2s and 14% of DEs. Furthermore, the largest group of regular wine drinkers is those aged between 35 and 49, with 34% of this group claiming they had drunk wine in the last week, as opposed to the smallest category, 18 to 24 year olds, of whom only 22% drank wine in the last week (weekly drinkers) (PAS Drinks Market Survey, 1994; © Public Attitude Surveys Ltd).

The statistics appear to confirm the suspicions already held by many, that wine drinkers are generally middle class and middle aged. But given that this market sector already occupies an established position as important restaurant consumers, this should be neither surprising nor a cause for concern. What needs to be discovered is what can be established about rather more specific market sectors and about attitudes to particular wines. In the first instance statistics seem to be able to give some fairly strong indications.

Male vs female wine drinkers

Not surprisingly men and women show rather different behaviour when it comes to their consumption of alcohol and wine. Men are more frequent drinkers than women. Of men 72% claim they drink alcohol (all forms) weekly as opposed to 50% of women and a higher proportion claim that they never drink alcohol at all (20% women and 14% men). In terms of both age and gender more British adults are becoming teetotal with a rise in total adult teetotallers of around 5% between 1980 and 1994 (PAS Drinks Market Survey 1994, © Public Attitudes Surveys Ltd). Not only do men drink alcohol more frequently but they are also heavier users. Analysis of 'heavy users' shows that they are disproportionately concentrated among men for wine (over three bottles a month), draught beer (14 or more pints in the last week) and cider (one or more pints in the last week) (Target Group Index, © BMRB 1995).

In terms of what sort of wine they like to drink, women are very strongly white wine drinkers. Of those women who had drunk wine in the last week, 65% claimed to have drunk white, while the figure for men was only 35%. The figures for red wine are not far from gender equality with those who claim to have drunk red wine in the last week being split almost down the middle at 51% men and 49% women (PAS Drinks Market Survey 1994, © Public Attitudes Surveys Ltd).

A survey by *Decanter* magazine (Neill, 1996: 50–51), discussed in greater detail below, also shows some of the attitudes which women have towards buying wine. When it comes to choosing wine, 'most women would prefer to make the decision themselves – 66 per cent feel comfortable choosing wine themselves, and 68 per cent are quite prepared to seek help from the restaurant wine waiter'.

The survey also found that women were most likely to find out about wine tips from their friends, with 79% getting their information that way. Only 38% of women were influenced by newspapers and 28% by glossy magazines. The most likely basis for their choice of wine was whether it would go with the food they were having and 65% bought it from supermarkets. An anomaly was the discovery that while 62% of women thought they knew at least as much about wine as men, 50% thought men were better at buying it (Neill, 1996: 51).

Wine use by country

Here again we find interesting trends emerging (Figure 2.4). Of those who drink Bulgarian wine the split appears to be a gender equal 50% men and a 50% women. The clear message here might well be that the easy drinking style, strong brand image and value for money offered by these wines is appealing irrespective of the sex of the drinker.

Other than this one notable example, women have the upper hand by a clear margin when it comes to enjoying wine. Clearly their most popular countries are Germany and Italy; of those who had drunk German or Italian

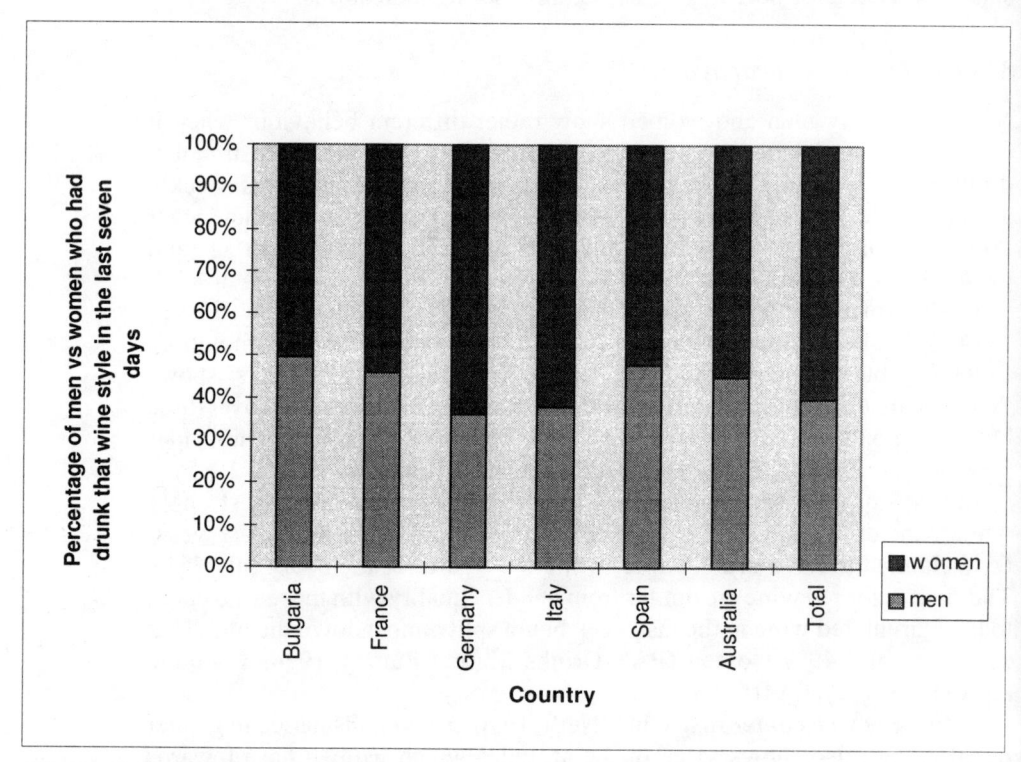

Figure 2.4 Profile of wine drinkers' gender by country of origin of the wine.
Source: PAS Drinks Market Survey 1994, © Public Attitudes Surveys Ltd; *The Drink Pocket Book* (1996: 105).

wine in the previous week 64% and 62% were women respectively.

Class and wine

At the opening to this chapter it was suggested that there is a tendency to correlate certain stereotypical characters with specific wines. In the section on consumer attitudes to wine later in this chapter I will explain why I think it is very difficult to gain a clear understanding of which wines are favoured by which socio-economic categories, but in the meantime it is worth trying to see whether any obvious trends exist.

Socio-economic group AB has already been identified as containing the most frequent wine drinkers, and statistics invariably show a gradual decline in wine drinking frequency in progress towards groups D and E.

As well as consuming more wine than those in lower socio-economic groups, the ABs consume different wines. Results (again from so-called 'seven day drinkers' – those who had consumed wine in the week before they were questioned) indicated that wealthier consumers were the predominant drinkers of wines from Australia, France and Bulgaria, while those in lower socio-economic groups preferred German and Italian wines (see Figure 2.5).

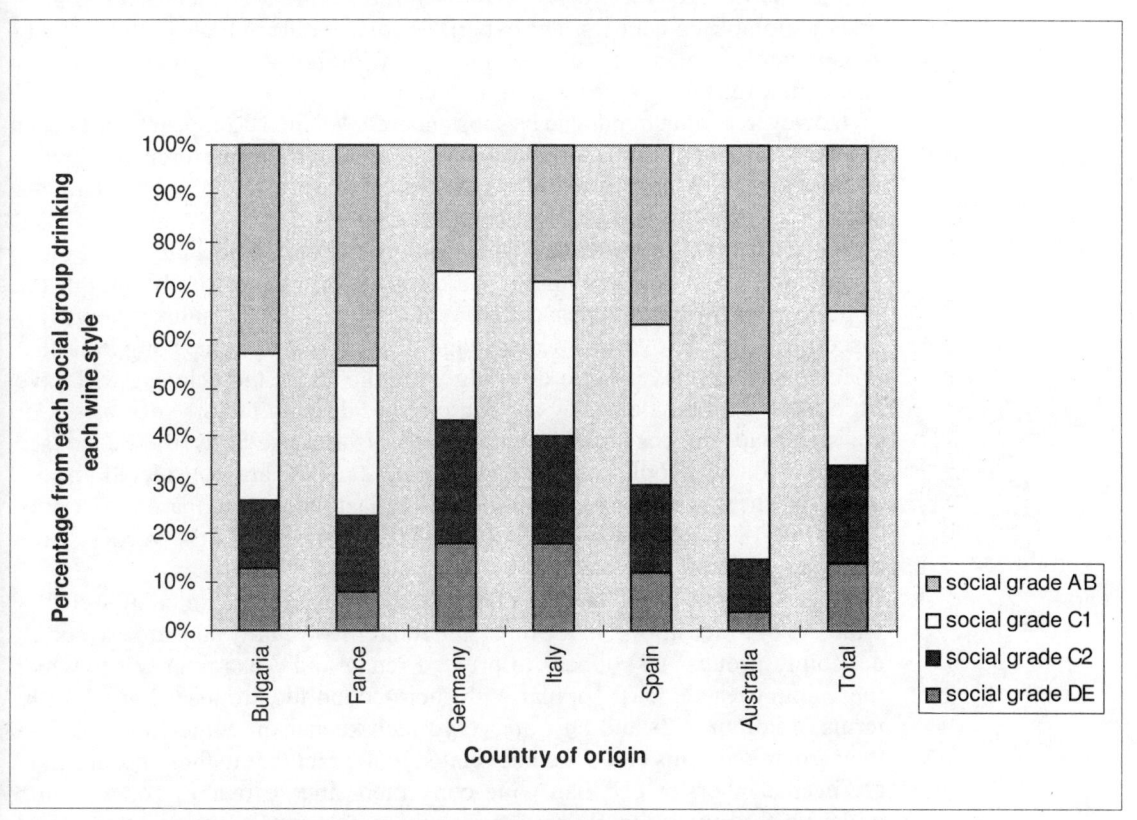

Figure 2.5 Profile of the social grade of wine drinkers by country of origin. Source: PAS Drinks Market Surveys 1994, © Public Attitudes Surveys Ltd; *The Drink Pocket Book* (1996: 105).

There could be several reasons for these differing consumption patterns. One is that the countries most favoured by those in groups A and B are major producers of premium wines which tend to be more expensive and are from countries with reasonably strong currencies, limiting the scope for selling discount products for merchants and restaurants. Alternatively the importance of female consumers may be clearer in the lower socio-economic groups. Certainly among men, beer drinking is far more popular in groups C2 and D than it is in groups A and B. A gradual rise in the proportion of men drinking beer as opposed to wine as one moves down the socio-economic scale would account for such a pattern.

Wine styles

Ultimately the most important issue for the restaurateur is what wine styles are likely to be wanted by the different consumer groups. Anyone who has spent time selling or dealing with wine professionally will certainly have come across people with hard and fast 'rules' about who drinks what. While many of these assertions may be true, one should be wary of taking seriously the prejudices of others. Much of what is believed about the type of person who drinks a particular wine is derived from a limited number of memorable brands and memorable consumers. The experience of a couple of nights spent serving large quantities of champagne to a table of 'wide-boys' could brand it forever as a 'drink for flashy types with too much money'.

However, certain trends can be substantiated. Women do appear to be keener drinkers of white wine and rosé than red, although the preference is by no means extreme. Men tend to prefer red wine over white and rosé, but again the preference is noticeable but not absolute.

Earlier it was suggested that wine drinking tended to be a pursuit of older people and this is backed up by market statistics. Interestingly though the popularity of different wines, differentiated by colour or country, shows few discernible trends over the various age groups. This perhaps suggests that once consumers have begun drinking wine the styles they choose will have little to do with how old they are and more to do with factors such as sex or class. Perhaps the one large exception to this is the case of fortified wine (see Figure 2.6). Of people over the age of 65, 213,000 are considered 'heavy users' of sherry (one or more glasses in the last week), compared with only 18,000 of 18 to 24 year olds. Those over 65 even outclass the keenest wine drinkers, 35 to 49 year olds.

Class certainly does have an effect on the consumer's choice of styles of wine. As outlined above, in the most general terms wealthy consumers (socio-economic groups AB) appear to prefer French and Australian wines while these countries are least popular with socio-economic groups C2 and DE. In terms of colour, C2s and DEs are very much keener on white and rosé than they are on red. This could well be related to the fact that in these groups men are beer drinkers rather than wine consumers and so overall consumption will tend to display female patterns for the whole group

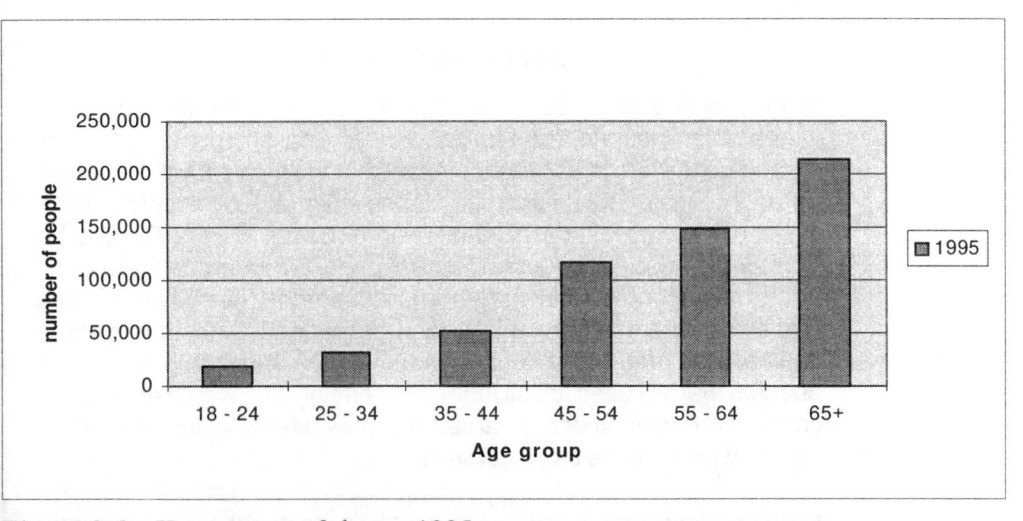

Figure 2.6 Heavy users of sherry, 1995.
Source: Target Group Index, © BMRB 1995, *The Drink Pocket Book* (1996).

NEW CONSUMER ATTITUDES TOWARDS WINE

In 1960 the *Economist* declared 'the British are at last becoming wine-drinkers' (cited in Barr, 1988: 4). The article explained that this was because public houses had begun selling wine and because sherry, as a standard branded product, had been heavily advertised in the 1950s. This meant that women, particularly from the middle class, who previously drank gin, could now enjoy a glass of wine. In retrospect this article was published at the start of the modern wine revolution, where it changed from being a prestige product for the privileged few in society to one generally consumed by the majority. Ironically, branded sherry, which did a great deal to generate widespread consumption of wine, now suffers from a poor public image, ageing consumers and declining market share.

During the 1960s the revolution in the consumption of 'light' or unfortified table wines began to take off. The catalyst for this was branded wines that could be advertised and sold as a standard product. Harvey's of Bristol was the first to launch a branded table wine range called 'Club', which did not succeed because it proved to be too expensive for most consumers. Part of the reason for this was because the product was advertised on television, with the costs of the campaign being recovered in the 16-shilling price of each bottle. To be commercially viable a branded wine needed to appeal to the wealthy working class and 16 shillings was just too much for them. However, what the Harvey's 'Club' range did achieve was to overcome one of the main consumer objections to buying wine at that time. Even today people are wary of new wines because they consider them an inconsistent product. While vintage variation and the nuances which make producers distinctive may delight connoisseurs, they are abhorred by ordinary consumers. Throughout this book the same issue crops up again and again – consumers are afraid of making mistakes and like to return to what they know best. In the early 1960s 'Club'

> **WHAT'S IN A NAME?**
>
> In the world of wine sales rather a lot it — certainly the appeal of wines from Australia, the USA and other English speaking nations — appears to stem in part from the fact that they have English names. To a UK consumer a name like 'Jacob's Creek' or 'Penfold's' is far easier to remember than an unfamiliar one such as 'Bereich Bernkastel' from Germany or 'Vacqueyras' from France. Furthermore there is the added disincentive that they might mispronounce the name and embarrass themselves. In the case of branded wines it is hard to estimate the effect of an English name, given the large promotional budgets that are used to sell them, but certainly one would expect that considerable customer appeal lies in names like 'Blue Nun' and 'Black Tower' which can be easily remembered.
>
> An interesting case of how the name of a wine might affect consumer appeal is that of the cult New Zealand wine 'Cloudy Bay'. I was once discussing this wine with a customer who remembered a competition to find the most beautiful phrase in the English language. The winner was apparently 'cellar door' — the combination of the graphic image it conjured up, the poetic metre with which it was said and its sound all contributed to its beauty. Interestingly the name 'Cloudy Bay' has all the same qualities.

wines contributed to the democratization of wine drinking by demonstrating that a new and more consistent type of wine was needed if wine merchants and restaurateurs were to persuade consumers to change to drinking wine. A more recent example of this policy has been the success of Australia as a light wine producer which regularly produces easy drinking wines with recognizable names and very little vintage variation.

The decline of the 'wine snob'

The success of Harvey's Club and the subsequent achievements of Australia and a number of other 'New World' producers with similarly consistent climates give us some indication of what factors go towards satisfying the modern wine consumer:

- consistency;
- brand;
- brand loyalty and brand identity.

Consistency

A move towards to a consistent product has been seen in a variety of products in recent years and wine is no different. Wine producers (and merchants) have always told their consumers that wine is an agricultural product and that they must simply accept the vagaries of nature. Lovers of wine from the classic producer regions of France and Germany have long put up with wines that are superb and abundant one year and thin, watery and in small quantities the next.

But wine like many other agricultural products has been forced to adapt to a changing market. Supermarkets now stock consistently high quality vegetables throughout the year and not surprisingly consumers expect the same from wine. As long as these wines are to their taste they are not over-selective about where they originate. Wine lovers of a former age (wine snobs) wanted wines from classic European regions with famous names. But in the same way that they do not mind whether their vegetables come from Zimbabwe or Israel, modern wine consumers increasingly do not object because their consistently good quality wine comes from Australia or Chile.

Brand

Although Harvey's Club was not a run-away commercial success, it did initiate a method of branding wine which was successful. Many consumers had not grown up in families which drank wine regularly. The first wines that they enjoyed were easily recognizable brands such as Mateus Rosé, Black Tower or Piat D'Or. Quickly identifiable by their names, bottle shapes and labels and remarkably consistent, these wines are as consumer friendly as Coca-Cola, and often as easy to drink.

Brand loyalty and brand identity

Wine drinkers have always liked to ally themselves to one sort of wine or another. Claret, burgundy, port and champagne all carry specific brand identities with which consumers are keen to associate. Many newcomers to the shelves of wine merchants/supermarkets and wine lists also have such identities. More tellingly, people attribute certain qualities to their peers on the basis of their wine choice.

Decanter magazine (Neill, 1996: 50–51) published a survey to discover whether women judged men by the wines they bought/drank. The survey interviewed 'professional women' across a range of age groups, of whom 63% said that they judged a man by the wine he bought (see Table 2.1).

The findings showed the respondents applying some very distinct characteristics to wines and their drinkers. As Richard Neill, author of the *Decanter* survey put it:

> Champagne man is a party lover but could be a Hooray Henry; Claret man is sophisticated but could be arrogant and snobbish; Burgundy man has all the advantages of sophistication without the drawbacks of Claret; Australian Chardonnay man is a sexy and adventurous new man; Chianti man is middle-of-the-road verging on boring and Rioja man is a raunchy party lover. However, if you thumb down the wine list and end up picking out a

Table 2.1 Wine and the man, the professional woman's view

%	Champagne	Claret	Burgundy	Californian Cabernet	Australian Chardonnay	New World Sparkling	Liebfraumilch	Chianti	Rioja
Sexy	38	6	6	16	16	4	–	10	10
Sophisticated	44	47	49	7	9	4	–	6	15
Arrogant	18	25	9	3	–	3	3	–	1
Mean	–	–	–	–	1	21	37	13	3
Boring	3	25	9	4	9	1	40	16	16
New Man	7	6	9	25	31	21	–	10	3
Hooray Henry	28	15	7	4	10	–	–	–	–
To be avoided	1	–	–	4	–	6	75	4	1

Source: *Decanter* (Neill, 1996: 50–51).

rather nice Liebfraumilch, don't be surprised if your date has vanished when you get back from the gents – she will already have marked you down as mean, boring and, most likely, a train-spotter or an Essex man.

This survey raises some interesting questions as to whether wine waiters and waitresses should attempt to identify what sort of customer they are dealing with and advise them accordingly. Probably not. The personae adopted by restaurant customers are complex and dependent upon mood, the purpose for dining out and their companions. In this context, pop psychologists applying consumer typologies to their customers are at best commercially ill advised. Where these findings may well be useful is in writing your wine lists. If Champagne is known to be seen as sexy then play on that and make the customer aware. If Burgundy is considered sophisticated then tell the world in your wine list. Like some of the best advertising, sell these products on the core brand values that already exist, rather than trying to invent spurious values to attach to them.

A second part of the *Decanter* magazine survey looked at what impressed women about their date's wine choice (see Table 2.2).

Well, 72 percent of women are impressed by a man who knows his wine regions, and 70 per cent go weak at the knees if you know how to match the wine to food.

The number one *faux pas*, however, is to base your selection on financial criteria.

These findings (Table 2.2) show one very important lesson for the wine waiter who wants to succeed. Do not be too impressive. One sure way to lose male customers is to demonstrate an encyclopaedic wine knowledge that lets you match food and wine perfectly ... and sends their partners away all starry eyed and sweet on you.

Table 2.2   Wine choice

%	Very impressed	Moderately impressed	Not at all impressed
Knowledgeable choice	72	28	–
Price/extravagance	–	33	67
Good match with food	70	30	–
Consulting you	42	39	19
Consulting the wine waiter	7	65	26

Source: *Decanter* (Neill, 1996: 50–51).

The results also produce another important finding. While two-thirds of respondents were 'moderately impressed' by men who consulted the wine waiter, only 7% were 'very impressed' and a quarter were 'not at all' impressed'. Although only speculation, this may be because consulting with the wine waiter is seen as an admission that one has a poor wine knowledge or lacks confidence. This sort of view must be overcome, not least because by consulting with a wine waiter/waitress the customer presents an opportunity to be 'sold to'. This allows good staff the chance to 'modify' the customer's choice to a wine that better matches the food, offers better value or, if one is mercenary, a bigger margin.

These factors together are creating what many would call the 'modern wine consumer'. Whereas 'traditional' snobs, certainly in the public imagination, restricted themselves to prestige, old world producer regions, modern consumers recognize the quality and values associated with such wines but do not feel that they should restrict themselves to these wines only. This is partly because there is no longer the belief that more expensive wines are necessarily better. In fact the results from the *Decanter* survey show that for some consumers spending a great deal on a bottle of wine is a positive turn-off. Furthermore modern consumers do not want to be restricted to one wine, and thus one brand image.

The new wine consumers – what do they look like?

Taking all these findings into account we can begin to build up an image of the sort of people to whom restaurants have to sell their wine. In the most general terms they constitute a far more broadly based cross-section of the population than perhaps forty or fifty years ago. The structure of the population has also changed considerably during that period, perhaps acting as a catalyst for changes in the wine drinking habits of the nation. Not only are more people wine drinkers, but they are regular drinkers. Wine has moved very firmly away from being a special occasion drink to a regular pleasure for millions and part of everyday life.

A picture emerges of a wine consumer who for the most part enjoys the consistency, as well as the easy drinkability of wine from many New World and particularly southern hemisphere countries. Andrew Barr identifies drinkability as a key factor in the modern fashion for wine drinking in the UK:

> The success of wine, though ostensibly due to the disappearance of snobbery, really is the reflection of another sort of social snobbery. The snobbery of one generation has been replaced by that of another: the snobbery of lightness. The closer an alcoholic drink product approaches fruit juice or water, the more we seem to prefer it.
>
> (Barr, 1988: 17)

These wines have no particularly strong brand connotations, making them a 'safe' purchase in the company of new acquaintances. Wines with anodyne or weak brand images also have the benefit that they can easily become everyday products. Earlier I mentioned that wine consumers are moving away from a view of wine as an everyday drink towards one where it is simply a part of everyday life. Certainly one could argue that part of the success of New World wines is that they do not carry messages of sexiness or sophistication – they are simply drinks to be enjoyed.

However, in the same way that consumers feel safe buying New World wines, there are occasions when they like to be able to communicate messages about themselves or project an image through the purchase of certain wines. So if they want to be sexy and opulent then they buy champagne; if they want to be sophisticated they choose burgundy. While Britain as a nation may have moved away from a situation where wine is viewed as a special occasion drink that can only be enjoyed when out at a restaurant, there are certain wines that retain an air of exclusivity. Proof of this can be seen in the way that television and film-makers use constant, feckless everyday enjoyment of 'special' wines as a means of demonstrating the fantastic wealth and conspicuous consumption of their characters.

And in the future?

The one largest trend that leisure analysts identify as affecting the restaurant/leisure market over the coming years is that of our ageing population. Within the leisure sector the main source of demand growth will come from the 40 to 64 year old age group. Not only will these people account for up to a third of the UK population by the year 2000, they are also the same people who have powered the wine boom for the last 20 years. They exhibit certain characteristics that would certainly warm the heart of those who want to sell good wine to affluent customers (Slattery *et al.*, 1996: 5).

- As their children have left home they have a high discretionary income which rises further as their mortgages get paid off. Furthermore these have often been (and remain) dual-income families.
- They already have stereos, televisions, microwaves and tumble dryers and tend to be contented with those they have – this means that on break-down the machine is replaced with an equivalent rather than the latest model, saving more money to be spent outside the home.
- Increasingly this powerful market sector is turning to leisure outside the home (including eating in restaurants). Dining out is a hedonistic and innately pleasurable activity, encouraging the consumer to do it again. The main restrictions on these enjoyable leisure activities have been lack of money and children at home, neither of which affect a growing proportion of the 40 to 65 age group.
- Finally, out-of-home leisure is by its very nature a public activity and involves public consumption. How often people dine out, where they dine and what they eat and drink when they get there are all lifestyle choices and are done to enhance standard of living and to give messages about how the person wishes to be seen in the world. If the purchase of certain wines is seen as giving off desirable messages about a person then one might reasonably expect the increasingly affluent 'late-middle-aged' increasingly to purchase these wines.

We are about to move into an era where the most powerful consumers are the 'Australian Chardonnay generation'. Yet this need not mean that nobody will drink the old classic wines from France's traditional regions. These consumers will buy wines to suit their mood. If they want an everyday wine then they will buy one, if they want something special, then they know enough about wine to ask for it confidently and they have enough money happily to pay for it.

The challenge for the restaurateur comes in being able to sell it to them. These are consumers who have worked hard for their money and are determined to enjoy their leisure. Also they have been brought up with wine and cannot be fobbed off with poor quality, overpriced wines acting as a cash cow to keep an ailing restaurant afloat. Well-costed, well-chosen, well-written wine lists are the order of the day. Hopefully the next few chapters of this book will tell you how to produce them.

QUESTIONS AND EXERCISES

1. Write down what you think the 'character' of the following wines is, or whether you think they have a character at all:
   - Port
   - Burgundy
   - Chilean Cabernet Sauvignon
   - English Müller-Thurgau
   - Piesporter

2. Pick three different people, maybe colleagues, television characters or lecturers and describe what sort of wine you think they would drink. Describe whether there are any other drinks you can imagine them enjoying. Ask yourself why you chose those wines/drinks.
3. Why do people drink champagne at weddings?
4. From what you have learnt in this chapter, what steps could the restaurateur take to promote a restaurant to romantic couples?
5. Is an ageing population that 'discovered' wine a good or a bad thing for those who sell wine?

FURTHER READING

When young trainees arrive for their first day at marketing companies and advertising agencies I am told that they are warned to beware of 'the sample of one' – that is to give too much credence to their own hunches and opinions about consumer preferences, when they are not supported by properly carried out statistical evidence. The reality for small restaurateurs is that, unassisted by large marketing budgets, the only market research that they are likely to be able to afford about the preferences of their customers is 'the sample of one', or possibly a friendly chat with some regular wine-loving customers.

Part of the reason for this dearth of information is that it is commercially valuable to those companies that commission it and frequently expensive to carry out. In the absence of specific research, I would recommend the *The Drink Pocket Book*, published annually by NTC Publications in association with Stats MR. For a more historical view consult *The Story of Wine* by Hugh Johnson (1989).

PART 2

Selection, purchasing and control

Choosing wines for a restaurant | 3

> **Key concepts**
>
> The main concepts in this chapter are:
> - sensory evaluation of wines;
> - relative worth;
> - commercial viability of wines.

INTRODUCTION.

Buying wine is not difficult. Although everyone has personal preferences, most people can distinguish a good wine from a bad one. Even those who only ever drink white wines out of choice, if pressed can say, 'Yes, this is a good red wine'. They can tell that it has no obvious chemical or 'off' aromas, that it is not overtly acidic or bitter and that it has a pleasant fruity taste. With practice this skill extends until they can say 'This is a good Chianti', knowing what particular characteristics are looked for in such a wine.

This chapter is about using this basic skill, identifying a good wine from a bad one when choosing wines for a restaurant list. Now it could be asked why a whole chapter is needed on this subject if it is so easy. The reason is that, as the first two chapters have already identified, the choice of wines available in the UK is vast. To try and make sense of the myriad choices needs a methodical approach. Each wine must be judged on its merits alone, not on the ambience of the surroundings when tasting it.

Take an example of what can happen when an ad hoc approach to wine buying is used. The policy of certainly larger restaurants and hotels is often to buy wine from a number of different merchants. It is often common sense not to put total faith in a single supplier. However, each of these suppliers will be vying for an ever larger chunk of the list so as to increase their business. To achieve this merchants will give tastings to show off a selection of their wines, perhaps accompanied by lunch or in pleasant surroundings. Under these circumstances it is all too easy to become carried away with the wines on offer. Back at the restaurant, when the wines are tasted again they can appear poor value for money or at worst faulty in some way. The restaurateur will wonder how such problems were dismissed quite so lightly, won over on polite chat and canapés.

This chapter is about adopting a methodical and almost scientific approach to tasting wine. Armed with knowledge and tasting notes that are unbiased and reliable, restaurateurs can assess the same or differing styles of wine against each other in terms of relative worth and consider the commercial viability of a style of wine within their particular restaurant. If the chapter could be said to have a general theme, particularly in the light of so many books and guides to wine tasting, it is that restaurateurs need to view each wine in a much broader context.

Wine tasting can become a very isolated business. Wines are considered one by one against each other and each is judged entirely in vinous terms. If restaurant wine buyers do this, they may well end up with a fascinating wine list full of interesting wines, but totally wrong for the restaurant. In choosing wines for a wine list buyers must constantly refer back to their final use. When people eat out it is to enjoy a harmonious whole – the meal experience. Wines chosen with this in mind will be chosen to match foods, not clash, to be good 'food wines', not characterful wines capable of masking or dominating the food.

SENSORY EVALUATION OF WINES

For the customer, one of the pleasures of wine is that they can be as knowledgeable or as ignorant as they like. For some wine is simply a question of finding what they like and coming back for more. For others it becomes an all-embracing hobby, involving house alterations to build cellars and taking all holidays in producing regions. Unfortunately many restaurateurs have also taken this viewpoint. If they like wine they will put a lot of effort into selling it. If not they will do the minimum required to build up a wine list that needs scant attention. I use the word unfortunately because wine is more than a hobby for restaurateurs, it is their business and as a business requires a serious approach.

The approach used within the wine trade to allow people to analyse wines is based around dividing up a wine by the senses. First its colour and appearance is noted, then its smell, and finally how it tastes and feels in the mouth. By recording a wine's qualities at each stage, tasters can then use their notes either as an aide-mémoire to recall a specific wine from the vast numbers often on show at a tasting, or to compare it against another when evaluating wines for a list. This is made easier by using the same terms or vocabulary to describe specific colours, smells and tastes which any taster will build up over time.

Tasting terms

There are few figures more easily satirized than television and newspaper wine pundits. Unfortunately for them they are caught between using flowery and obtuse terms in an attempt to make a wine sound as interesting as it tastes and failing to interest their readers and viewers. Terms like 'wheelbarrow loads of ugli fruit' may well amuse those who read wine columns and watch television wine recommendations, but few would be inspired to buy a wine because someone said that it tasted 'nice'.

Those buying wine for a restaurant should remember that these terms often owe rather more to literature and creative English than the genuine first impressions of the wine in a tasting room. Analytical wine tasting, or oenology, is ultimately a scientific skill which uses that most sensitive piece of equipment, the nose, to detect specific chemicals in wines. The smells and tastes are evocative of more or less specific product. Thus a vanilla taste in wine derives from vanillin, a by-product of barrel ageing. Cabernet Sauvignon is identified by its cassis or blackcurrant aroma, Gewürztraminer by its characteristic lychee smell. Thus, an initial troublesome grasping for the words to describe a wine, particularly with those already familiar with the main terms used in the tasting room, will lead with practice to a reasonably consistent use of a vocabulary that not only genuinely describes to you what a wine tasted like, but also even to others.

The paraphernalia of wine tasting

Wine books often devote a great deal of space to the importance of pristine tasting rooms, ideal glasses and the rules and etiquette of wine tasting. In truth, worries about whether wines are being tasted in perfect conditions for objective analysis are the domain of oenologists and keen amateurs. Most wine merchants and restaurateurs are far too busy to spend time worrying about the trivialities of tasting, they do it 'on the hoof'. By this I mean that it is all very well to be told that tastings should take place in south facing, airy rooms with plenty of natural light and banks of white Formica tables, but often there is simply not the opportunity.

The most important thing to remember is to try to remain objective. It is unwise to commit yourself to buying wine on the impressions gained at a sociable gathering. People often tell of wines that tasted superb when they bought them in France on holiday but were at best ordinary when they arrived home. This is not an example of a wine that did not travel well, but rather of how much influence one's state of mind can have on impressions of taste. As mentioned at the beginning of this chapter, merchants always try to increase the number of their wines on restaurant lists. They know that the wines invariably taste superb after a few glasses of champagne and lunch and so many choose to present them in this way. Restaurateurs who are not cautious can soon find they have a burgeoning wine list filled with ordinary wines. The problems are compounded by the difficulty of having to keep track of dozens of suppliers and accounts and remembering what is ordered from whom.

Wine tasting and note taking

There are as many schools of thought on wine tasting notes and score cards as there are people who use them. Some use numerical scores, while others regard

WINE TASTING

For a cautious restaurateur a few simple rules when at wine merchant's tastings can make all the difference between buying a solid list of saleable wine and overfilling the wine list with wine chosen in the heat of the moment.

- Either enjoy a merchant's tasting as a harmless day out or as a serious opportunity to select wines for your list, not both.
- Try to taste different wines for your list in similar circumstances, using the same style of glasses (ISO approved are ideal), and accompanied by your own thoughts, not those of a salesman.
- Avoid using perfumed deodorant, aftershave, perfumes, make-up, hairspray or gel. Even something relatively innocuous like lip balm can affect your perception of the wines as well as the perception of those around you.
- Sometimes try to taste wines blind. In restaurants many wines are sold initially on their name or appellation, but repeat purchases are made on their true quality. Don't be led astray by a fancy label or well-known name.
- Taste hungry. Taste buds are far more sensitive before a meal and several hours after the last one. A break from eating will also get rid of any residual flavours of food (or toothpaste) from your mouth that might affect tasting.
- Take notes. The effort of thinking of words to describe the taste will help you to concentrate. For restaurateurs this is especially important because if they later buy the wine it may have to be described on a list or to staff, when the initial tasting notes will prove invaluable.

it as impossible to put a score on a wine. Some of those who score their wines go to one hundred and some to ten. Some like to use preprinted cards with suggestions and spaces for specific remarks, while others like to formulate their own notes, writing almost in an essay style.

Whatever method is chosen is immaterial, so long as notes are taken and can be referred back to later. In this context later may mean the next day when attempting to decide which Côte-Rôties from the various suppliers sampled is going on the list. Alternatively it may mean several years later when you suspect the quality of a house wine has changed and wish to refer to your original tasting notes to see what they said.

In writing notes use the style that comes most easily and stick to it. Concise notes written on one day and flowery essays the next may swing your judgement in favour of the more comprehensively described wine. Finally, read other people's note-taking style and tips. Two outstanding books for learning about this are Michael Broadbent's *Pocket Guide to Wine Tasting* (1982) and the more oenologically based *The Taste of Wine* by Emile Peynaud (trans. Michael Schuster, 1987). Both of these books give a great insight into developing tasting skills and describing what you taste; anyone who wishes to expand their skills will find them invaluable. However, without going into too much detail it is worth briefly covering the basic technique used.

Wine tasting: appearance

If nouvelle cuisine did anything for food it was to develop the idea of eating with our eyes before we eat with our mouth. Food that looks foul has to taste superb to win over the impression left by its appearance. The same is true of wine. Wine that is cloudy or filled with bits is immediately treated with caution. Yet a clear glossy appearance with a rich colour is instantly appealing.

When learning about wine tasting, the description of the appearance is the easiest part to learn. Humans have very good eyesight and use it far more than their sense of smell or even taste. If a wine looks good it is easy to spot. When writing notes things to jot down are the clarity of the wine from distinctly dirty, cloudy or just hazy, to a bright or brilliant lustre. It is worth noting the viscosity of the wine – usually by looking at the alcohol tears or 'legs' that run down the sides of the glass after swirling the wine. These tears are often cited as a method of telling how unctuous a wine will be either through high alcohol or residual sugar left after fermentation. Either way the feel of the wine in your mouth is a rather more reliable indication of this. At this stage it is also worth noting if there are any bubbles or a slight fizz (spritz) in the wine. In many light whites and reds this spritz can add a pleasant 'lift', particularly if they lack a little acidity.

Finally, consider the colour of the wine. On the whole as long as this is appealing and rich that is fine. With other factors such as aroma, the colour of the wine can give a lot away about a wine, which is particularly useful in wine trade exams or dinner party blind-tasting games. For the restaurateur, as long as the wine is not going brown (oxidizing) before its time and does not appear too watery, for the most part appealing colour means appealing wine.

Wine tasting: smell

It comes as a surprise to many to discover that much of what we regard as the 'taste' of a wine is actually its smell. To confirm this just try drinking a glass of wine with a clip on your nose. Then try the same wine with your nose clear and notice how many more flavours you can distinguish. Often nuances in a wine are undetected if it is merely drunk, that become clear when gently inhaled through the nose.

To pick out these smells take a glass and concentrate as you take your first sniff. It is in this first sniff that most will be revealed about the wine. Later sniffs may reinforce an initial impression, but first impressions remains the most informative. Many people wildly slosh their wine around before they have had a gentle nose at it. This is a mistake as they lose many of the subtler aromas that contribute to its quality. After gaining an initial impression, have a swirl and try to pick out further aromas from the wine

By following the instructions of wine books too closely, it is easy for a restaurateur to become overinvolved in the detail of party game wine tasting, rather than looking for straight forward quality. Instead of attempting to dissect a wine too much, simply record on a tasting card what first comes to mind and leave any analysis until later.

First, look for how clean the flavour is. Make sure there are no smells you find unpleasant or out of place such as mould or a sharp piercing acidity. If the wine is 'clean', look for smell you do like. Does the wine have a particularly characteristic taste of a specific grape variety or some other very noticeable fruit aroma? If your list needs a classic Cabernet Sauvignon, does this one fit the bill or is it indistinguishable from so many other red wines? Look for other non-fruit smells, vanilla pointing to oak ageing, or the truffle and tar aroma of some north Italian reds. Consider how intense these smells are. If your restaurant is noted for powerful flavours in its dishes could a delicate wine (no matter how fine) stand up to the competition. Finally, in older wines consider the bouquet. Aroma is the term used to describe those clear-cut, often fruit flavours that derive from the grape itself. Bouquet refers to the subtler smells that come about when wines have been aged, either in oak or bottle. They are what lead people to describing a wine as having mellowed or softened with age. Whereas aroma thrusts out from the glass, each aroma identifiable in isolation, bouquet often takes time to evolve and acts less in isolation but as a harmonious whole.

Wine tasting: taste

Nobody quite knows how many smells humans can distinguish. Some claim that there is a set number, be it hundreds or tens of thousands. Others claim that the way the nose works puts no limits on the number of smells we can tell apart. We are limited merely by the number of aromas we come across. The same is not true of the tongue, which only has four tastes – sweet, salty, acid and bitter. No matter how complex a wine is, the tongue's four-taste limitation usually only serves to confirm what has already been smelt.

As the nose clip experiment points out though, taste in the mouth is not strictly limited to the four sensations of the tongue. The nose plays a vital part in 'tasting' a wine, as aromas from the mouth travel up into the nose from the back of the mouth, via the 'retronasal' route. For the restaurateur, the wine is being tasted not to pick out wines for 'grapies' to enthuse over, but for customers to enjoy with a meal. Restaurant customers may gently take in the aroma and bouquet of a wine, but for the most part it is there to be enjoyed with a meal. Thus when choosing a wine the actual taste and 'mouth feel' retain critical importance.

The actual process of tasting in the mouth is simple. Take a reasonable sip into your mouth so that you can work it around and move it across your tongue. This ensures that all the zones on your tongue from the sweet at the front, the acid at the side to the bitter at the back are covered. Chewing the wine, although seemingly a pointless exercise gives a great impression of the wines weight and 'texture' in the mouth. Draw a little air into your mouth by pursing your lips as if pronouncing an 'F' and sucking on a straw. This releases volatile aromas which move up into the nose. Drink a little. Although this may be impractical at a large tasting (and even dangerous if driving), the wine is being tasted to see if it is suitable to drink. Therefore it makes sense that you drink before buying. Finally spit out most of the wine. If all the wine from each sample is drunk, no authority can be given to your impressions of the various wines as the alcohol takes its inevitable effect. At very large tastings, even the smallest drink of each and every sample soon totals up. In these circumstances, the best policy is to go back later to those few wines that were most impressive. Many people initially underestimate the cumulative effect of a number of tasting measures. (At a large tasting I attended in London by the end of the day we were aware of an increasingly boisterous man at the back of the room. Eventually he told a very embarrassed woman next to him that he needed the lavatory. After knocking over his chair he set off for the door. The rest of us had just got back into the tasting when there was a massive crash – the unfortunate taster had concussed himself by walking into the doorframe.)

After spitting out the wine, do not forget about it. How does the flavour develop in the mouth? Does it linger pleasantly or is there an disagreeable aftertaste? How long does this last? Some measure this 'length' of a wine with a stopwatch. For the restaurateur it is enough to know that there is a pleasant lingering sensation after spitting.

Finally, consider the taste and take notes – from the 'attack' of the wine when it was taken into the mouth, through the development of flavours as it was swirled and chewed, to the finish, the combination of length, texture (mouth feel) and aftertaste.

General impressions

In Chapter 1 the division for many people between food and wine was discussed. All too often food and wine are considered in complete isolation without reference to each other. Quite why such natural partners should be seen in this way is perhaps a matter for sociologists, but for restaurateurs it is something to be resisted. Restaurateurs buy wines to be drunk with food. This may seem an obvious statement, but by tasting wines in many restaurants it would appear to be often ignored.

When making notes, especially when drawing conclusions, every effort should be made to put the wine in the context of its final use. Wines bought by restaurateurs will all be enjoyed with food, and specifically the style of food served in that restaurant. While a wine may taste superb on its own at a tasting, when drawing conclusions about whether to buy it always think in terms of how it would work with the proposed menu.

Wines that appeal to the senses in isolation can often be the very worst wines to match with food. Likewise, apparently characterless wines with little to recommend them, rather than entering into a battle for supremacy of the senses, blend and marry with foods to become ideal 'food wines'. Perhaps the finest examples of this come from Mediterranean countries with strong culinary traditions. Grape varieties such as Airén in Spain and Trebbiano in Italy are often criticized for producing large quantities of dull white wine. Yet both these countries also produce superb, powerfully flavoured wines that are ideal as 'drinking wines' or to be partnered with very specific foods. The dull whites are food wines, designed to add to a harmonious meal experience, not to fight for supremacy.

Conclusions

Wine tastings can be one of the great perks of owning or running a restaurant or hotel. Few other jobs allow people the chance to try ranges of fascinating and interesting wines for free, often in pleasant surroundings accompanied by lunch. But restaurateurs are only invited because the merchants covet their custom. If the restaurateurs' purpose is to buy for their lists they must be aware that the ambience may make the wines seem rather more appealing than they really are. If unsure, do not commit to take on the wines there and then. Instead take good notes and resolve to look at the wine again later, perhaps against comparative wines from other merchants in a more anodyne setting. When taking notes, remember their purpose. Many books on tasting are aimed at consumers – people who taste wine for a hobby. Their readership is not the restaurateur whose living depends to some extent on making the correct selection at this stage. Picture each wine with the menu. Consider how versatile it is. Would it appeal to few customers and suit one or two dishes, or to a broader audience and match a large proportion of the menu?

The actual mechanics of wine tasting, the skills necessary to build up an impressive, well thought out list, be it large or small, are relatively easy to learn. Each of us has the tools of a nose, mouth, and so on, and marshalling them properly takes only a few basic rules. The development of these skills is open to anyone with the time and inclination. Before long it becomes easy to pick out a few grape varieties and even styles of winemaking peculiar to specific countries. All this is useless to the restaurateur unless performed in the correct state of mind, constantly applying what the wine tastes like to its final use, and placing each wine in a broader context.

THE QUESTION OF RELATIVE WORTH

With the use of a nose, eyes and mouth that function reasonably well, plus a little practice, it is not difficult to find a range of good quality wines to fill a wine list. Reputable merchants would not attempt to sell anything that they knew to be faulty or really unpalatable. Wines chosen to accompany the menu are likely to provide good and sometimes outstanding matches to the foods. The next hurdle to cross is to ensure that these wines work financially. First, they must be marked up at a price which customers consider reasonable. Second, they must provide quality cheaply enough to give good margins to the restaurant.

It is easy to attend a tasting, identify most of the top quality wines and buy these for a list. A much harder task is to go to the same tasting and decide where similar levels of quality can be bought for a fraction of the price. Take an example. Chardonnay is a fairly ubiquitous grape variety on merchants' lists and is grown in almost every wine-producing country in the world. It is also reasonably versatile and can produce wines from good quality table wine to top notch Grand Cru, *appellation contrôlée*. This means that there are Chardonnays from £2 or £3 to over £100 on merchants' lists. The problem for restaurateurs is to decide, with their style of restaurant in mind, which of these provides value for money. For a very few restaurants with a wealthy clientele it maybe that their customers see Le Montrachet at £200 as a good buy. For most though, wines that are sold nearer the £15 mark are not going to be seen as only fractionally as good.

This is obviously an extreme example, but the principle holds true at all price levels. Given that the public are relatively sensitive on the subject of restaurant wine mark-up levels, it is very easy to become labelled as having an 'expensive wine list'. It is far better practice to be known for having a well thought out wine list with interest and quality at affordable levels than to be known for having all the world's great wines, at a price.

Alternatives and individuality

Although there are thousands of wines in the world and many of them come to Britain every year, one of the most surprising characteristics of restaurant wine lists is how similar they all look. Well-tried German medium whites, claret-style French reds and the same brands of overpriced champagne leave wine lovers and adventurous diners disappointed and bored. The laws of supply and demand inevitably account for this and these wines may be cheap and nasty or good and wildly overpriced. However, if producers and brokers find they can continue to sell on this basis why should they change?

To overcome this problem requires an open and inquisitive mind. Unlike many countries, Britain does have alternatives on the market. Given the ease with which merchants have continued to sell the same 'formula' lists to their clients, a little more work than usual may be required to create an interesting and exciting list. The interest that this will subsequently generate will certainly make the effort worthwhile.

Seeking value from merchants

This book does not intend to sound unduly harsh on the subject of wine merchants. If the wines they offer to restaurant clients are dull and repetitive this is because they are fulfilling the demands of their customers. However, sometimes it is necessary to be pushy or insistent to get the best value. Wine merchants will always attempt to increase their roster of restaurant clients, with the result that they have less time to devote to existing customers unless explicitly asked to do so. Thus when going to a merchant the restaurateur should be armed with a list of pertinent questions and tips on how to get value and quality over and above the usual restaurant list.

When choosing wines it is best to keep foremost the question: 'What alternatives are there in this quality bracket and how much do they cost?' Not only should you bear this in mind, but also ask the merchant the same question, frequently. The alternatives do not need to be exactly the same style of wine produced elsewhere. They may be a variation on a theme, a grape variety differently vinified or a previously unrecognized variety in a new growing area – but importantly they will be interesting and better value.

Unfortunately, if the rules of innovation and originality could be written down and learnt by all they would lose their value, but some general tips may be useful in identifying those wines that will set a list apart from the crowd.

- **Use tasting notes**. Even the simple act of writing things down usually helps people remember what they have learnt. If what is written down is easily available to refer to, all the better. Thus if at the nth tasting in a month you taste yet another Australian Chardonnay, the fact that you have taken notes on all the previous ones makes comparisons easier and assists selection of the one which is the best value.
- **Lesser known producers**. These are particularly pertinent when selecting wines from very well known areas like Burgundy or Bordeaux. The best producers know they can command high prices and will do so. Lesser known producers often have to fight harder for recognition and thus produce better quality wines for the money. Predictably though, this is not always an easy process and can require a certain amount of work by the restaurateur in reading wine columns or magazines or even just listening to the comments and recommendations of others.
- **Lesser known regions**. These can be particularly fruitful in classic producer nations like France, Spain or Italy where little-recognized producers work hard to sell their wines. Lacking the cachet of a well-known *appellation* these wines suffer in the marketplace. They can be made using soils, processes and grapes identical to the classic regions and are sometimes later 'discovered', becoming fashionably unsnobbish. Southern France, Italy and Valdepeñas in Spain are all examples of such regions.
- **Lesser known countries**. These can be broken up into various different categories. First, there are those long-standing producer nations which have started producing more quality wine for export, as opposed to bulk wine for the home market. Within these countries iconoclastic, adventurous domestic producers and 'flying winemakers' (overseas consultants bought in to supervise production) often provide stunning value and very individual wines. Examples of these countries are Portugal (for table wines), Chile and parts of Eastern Europe. The second category of country is those producing wine on a major commercial scale for the first time. The classic example of this has been New Zealand, whose small industry prior to the late 1980s has been transformed by its export success.
- **Declassified wines**. Distressingly, these wines are currently very fashionable and show few signs of becoming more reasonably priced in the near future. This said, as countries increasingly regulate their wine industries, placing greater emphasis on regional characteristics and style, there will always be producers willing to step outside the law and produce quality wines that fail to qualify for regulated names. The most famous examples of this school of winemaking are the 'Super Tuscans', the Sangiovese-based Italian reds led by Antinori's Sassicaia. Aimé Guibert's Mas de Daumas Gassac from

the South of France and Calo Falco's Marqués de Grignon from Rueda in Spain are now equally well-established classics, but have a host of imitators that is worthy of investigation by the restaurateur.

- **Oddities**. As a class this is understandably harder to define, but examples can show the sorts of wines to look for. Château Musar in the Lebanon produces a claret style of wine with plenty of ageing potential and cheaper than many comparable wines. Producers in many New World countries are increasingly using rare or even almost extinct grape varieties: Petit Syrah, the hearty Charbono, Beaujolais-like Tarrango, not to mention the now popular Viognier.
- **Be bold.** Go with your instincts, they are usually right. When tasting wines, especially at blind tastings, many people worry that they are going to look foolish if they choose the 'the wrong wine', favouring an unknown over something famous. If all the names on the wine list are familiar to the customers, unless very cheap they offer nothing new. The restaurant will be marked down as the same as the rest and not particularly good value. If a wine appeals to you at a blind tasting that later turns out to be an oddity, believe in your conviction. This will develop a list that is interesting and good value.

THE COMMERCIAL VIABILITY OF WINES

Having just extolled the virtues of being brave and choosing the weird and wonderful for a wine list, it will now appear contrary to claim that wines should be chosen on the basis of their commercial viability. Blind tasting with a merchant can only tell a restaurateur or manager what a wine tastes like – something that the customers are not going to do until they have identified the wine on the list, considered it suitable for the occasion and ordered it from the sommelier. If customers ask for advice it may be possible to steer them towards an unfamiliar wine, but this entails effort, time and sometimes considerable powers of persuasion – not to mention the disappointment if the unknown wine turns out to be something they do not like. In choosing wines for a list it is worth remembering that wines, like many other products, are brands and have a 'brand personality'. What wine you choose says a great deal about you and about the occasion. For non-experts keen to avoid looking lost with a list of unfamiliar names, a single wine they have heard of before and can pronounce is worth a whole list of superb but unknown wines. For those in the business of wanting to impress, good value falls by the wayside in favour of conspicuous consumption of the wines of famous domaines with expensive *appellations*.

For most restaurants the choice of a suitable wine list requires balance, and a little market research and knowledge of their customers. Restaurants specializing in fine food would be foolish to build up a list made up entirely of inexpensive, little known wines, irrespective of their intrinsic quality. Customers expect to be able to choose wines from the world's classic regions, not to be limited to the manager's favourites which they have never heard of. Conversely, bistro outlets targeting younger or more adventurous clients will find that an iconoclastic wine list will appeal to those who feel that the world's 'classic' regions, particularly in France, are overpriced.

Fashion, prestige and fame

Although there are probably a great many different ways of classifying the factors that make a wine (or any other product) commercially viable, the three which seem particularly pertinent to wine list selection are fashion, prestige and fame.

When restaurateurs seek out wines that carry these tags (fashionable, prestigious and famous) they must remember that they are very much 'added value' products. In totally blind tasting such wines might not show a flavour differential that would justify being several pounds to several times more expensive than their less famous, prestigious or fashionable competitors. But restaurateurs who ignored them on this basis would be extremely foolish. In the absence of being able to taste each and every wine, the customer has only two options in making a choice. The first is to ask advice from the restaurant staff and trust them to give good and knowledgeable recommendations. The second is to be presented with a list which offers a reasonable number of wines that the 'average customer' would be aware of and wish to buy. Each restaurant's 'average customer' is different but experience and research can help in building up a picture of what they enjoy and the core of the list must be built around the requirements and pockets of this market.

Fashion

Very fashionable wines are usually from new or revitalized wine regions and characterized by an imaginative use of marketing acumen. They may rise to prominence in a relatively short period of time and, increasingly, to use industry jargon, they are described as 'cult' wines.

It is perhaps easiest to describe some of these wines through examples, the most of which is the New Zealand 'cult' Sauvignon Blanc, Cloudy Bay. This wine is so sought after that it is sold on an allocation basis. In order to ensure a continuity of supply restaurants may well apply for allocations themselves, rather than relying on wholesaler's stocks which are liable to run dry before the next release. To some extent this winery can take the credit for making South Island New Zealand Sauvignon Blancs 'cult' wines generally. At the risk of overgeneralizing, the typical Cloudy Bay customer is a young to middle aged, middle-class professional who knows a reasonable amount about wine but enjoys the exciting, vibrant image of New World wines, in contrast to the 'dusty old Colonels' image of the classic regions of France. 'Typical' customers have gone beyond the standard Australian blends, but have a little more money to spend and so are looking for something rather more exclusive. Cult wines are an ideal marriage of a sense of connoisseurship with the less pretentious image of the New World that appeals to many wine drinkers today.

Fashionable wines are not confined to New Zealand or even the New World, although a great many of these wines do come from there. As countries like South Africa and Chile rise to prominence, it is worth looking out for wines from these countries that seem to receive much attention from the wine press. Given the very forward nature of these wines, with plenty of approachable fruit and clean well-structured flavours, they also appeal to the judges in wine competitions where a strong showing can almost guarantee commercial success and publicity.

There is a caveat though when developing a list that is strong on very fashionable wines. As with any added value product, this value only remains in place as long as the public still deems the image to be worth more than the sum of its intrinsic parts. These are not wines for those who want a minimal involvement list. Forethought and a real knowledge of what is happening in the wine trade are required to make the most of the opportunities offered by fashionable wines in order to capitalize on them, make money while the public is prepared to pay, and move on to new products when the time is right.

Prestige

Don't believe a word you hear about the death of the wine snob; snobs are alive and well and eating out in restaurants right across the country. Without wanting to dwell unduly on the sociology of the meal, people do not go to restaurants simply to stop themselves from feeling hungry. There may be a great many reasons why people dine out but often embedded somewhere is the desire to impress: to impress a business partner, a lover, a prospective lover or a future parent-in-law – it does not matter.

The choice of restaurant will be part of this attempt to impress, particularly if it has a good reputation for the quality of its food or wine list. Once inside the restaurant the main tool with which to create an impression is the wine list. Diners choose their own food from the menu, but the host is usually the only person to choose from the wine list. Discernment and taste must be displayed, not to mention generosity. Thorstein Veblen, considering nineteenth-century gentlemen in *The Theory of the Leisure Class*, wrote that in order 'to discriminate with some nicety between the noble and the ignoble in consumable goods' the gentleman of leisure 'becomes a connoisseur in creditable viands of various degrees of merit, in manly beverages and trinkets'(1899: 47). Most of those who choose the wine in modern restaurants are neither leisured nor exclusively men, but nonetheless great social currency is still placed on being able to make a knowledgeable choice. As most people are not great wine experts, they will be unwilling to take the risk of selecting an unfamiliar wine which turns out to suit nobody. Instead they will want to see a list of familiar names which conjure up images of rustic cellars, old barrels, and hearty vignerons hand-bottling their vinous nectar to be sold in exclusive restaurants.

Thus in some restaurants, particularly those with an expensive or sumptuous brand, it is worthwhile having a list which includes a good number of exclusive estates. By this I mean Premier and Grand Cru burgundies, 'First' and 'Super-Second' growth châteaux in Bordeaux and the Italian Super-Tuscans. They may appear to be prohibitively expensive, particularly after even a relatively modest mark-up and VAT, but for those buying them value for money is rarely the point. Real wine lovers are not the target market. They know that they can buy the wines for half the price at good wine merchants and enjoy them at own home in an atmosphere rather more conducive to the sort of

THE COMPLEX BUSINESS OF CLASSIFYING EXPENSIVE WINE

To the uninitiated the small changes in classification that indicate massive changes in price of the world's finest wines can appear illogical and very confusing. This impression derives from the fact that frequently these systems are illogical and almost deliberately confusing. Perhaps the most famous classification system of all is that found in the Médoc region of Bordeaux in South West France. This was devised in 1855 and ranks 60 Cru Classés (wines from different châteaux) into five separate classes. The 18 Crus Grands Bourgeois Exceptionnels, 41 Crus Grands Bourgeois and 68 Crus Bourgeois that sit below the Crus Classés are no longer allowed to use the terms on their labels and so are no longer seen. Unfortunately for the unwary wine buyer the Cru Classé terms that are still used are no longer totally reliable indicators of wine quality. The wines in the top or Premier Cru Classé can usually be relied upon to provide superb (frequently sublime) wine at a serious price, while those in the lower classes should be bought with more care as they frequently provide better drinking and better value for money than their counterparts in higher classes. Among the Second Growth wines are those, often referred to as 'Super-Seconds' which can command prices comparable to those of their top-class cousins.

Confusingly, the other great French wine-producing region, Burgundy, uses a different method of classifying its great wines altogether. While there is not room here to go into the complexities of the Burgundian vineyard ownership system, the top 1% or so of Burgundy production is sold as Grand Crus (Great Growths) followed by 600 Premier Crus (First Growths) about another 11% of production (Hanson, 1995: 6).

Finally it is worth mentioning the interesting case of the Italian 'Super Tuscans'. Faced with the very rigid confines of the Italian DOC classification system, innovative Italian wine producers have taken to ignoring this classification system altogether and producing wines that merely qualify for the status of 'table wine'. Reflecting the origin of most of these wines, certainly in the early days, the term 'Super Tuscans' has come to be applied to those wines often made with non-indigenous grape varieties that carry a humble label classification and a not so humble price.

chatter and debate that great wine lovers seek. Those who order prestigious wines in restaurants want to buy the aura and reputation that the names of the very best estates carry with them, their brand image of historical pastoral scenes, with hearty Frenchmen happily applying their craft to provide the wines for the world's rich.

With this 'brand image' in mind it is easy to understand the sort of wines that live in this category. While those previously described as 'fashionable' have an appeal that is new, media and market led and occasionally somewhat fleeting, these prestigious wines owe their appeal (and market value) to their sense of timelessness. As opposed to being market led they are 'history led' and will therefore never come from the New World. This sector of the wine market contains notable writers and 'gurus' such as Robert Parker from the USA. His *Wine Buyers Guide*, often referred to simply as 'Parker', was first published in Britain in 1989 and is now in its fourth edition (1996). Although a massive volume it concentrates entirely on the very best (and most prestigious) producers and their wines from around the world. Parker has a system of scoring wines on a scale of 1 to 100. Many, including those who enjoy the very best wines, place a great deal of trust in Parker and his scoring system, despite the controversy it raises among many wine lovers. These scores can 'make or break' wines, particularly those in contentious vintages, and cloud the judgement of those who see them on lists. Therefore, if a wine list is to include a great many top class wines, selection must be made with a certain degree of caution. It is not enough just to go for reasonable vintages and famous houses. Attention must be paid to those producers favoured by the guides, those vintages that are recommended, and these recommendations should be used either on the list or in speaking with customers.

Finally, although many restaurants would dearly like to feature the world's finest and most sought after wines, these must be viewed dispassionately and as any other tool of the business. The outlay on such wines can be considerable and unless there is a realistic chance that customers are going to choose them they will become nothing more than very expensive problems. If they will not sell the money is better spent on extra cases of house white to ensure that it never runs out. Certain types of people buy these wines, usually wealthy individuals who enjoy spending their money. Only experience and research will tell restaurateurs whether this is an accurate description of their clientele, and whether they may cautiously start to build up a selection of the very finest wines.

Fame

If the terms fashion, prestige and fame sound rather interchangeable this is because to some degree they are. But in broad and general terms, fashionable wines are found in talked about, exciting restaurants often with a fashionable image themselves. Prestigious wines are found in rather more staid restaurants, perhaps with a long reputation for excellence. Finally while the rather more interesting 'oddball' wines discussed earlier in the chapter should feature on any list that wants to be exciting and interesting, all lists are built around a core of famous names.

A strategy of choosing famous names serves a variety of purposes. First it means that within each of the various styles of wine, light red, heavy red, dry white, sweet white, there is a well-known wine that customers can choose without having to ask the sommelier and (in some eyes) appear foolish or unknowledgeable about wine. While it may be admirable to preach the virtues of brave and innovative wine choices to the converted, many people know the style they like and what it is called and want to be able to order it whenever they go out – and who can blame them.

For the restaurateur there are advantages in an approach that mixes the new and unknown with the famous. On the one hand the list will appeal to wine lovers who will (hopefully) talk about it, generating those word of mouth recommendations which are the best form of marketing. On the other hand the same list carries wines that the less daring want to buy. Customers will pay a premium for a wine choice that they know they will like and for the accompanying peace of mind. Less well known wines, although desirable, are harder to sell and may not be gross profit earners like the Piesporters and the Muscadets.

CONCLUSION

In choosing wines for a restaurant list bear two questions in mind. First, what does it taste like? To assess this, use the basic rules of tasting: look, smell, taste, spit and write. Always try to do this without the mental baggage of the wine's name to give you any preconceptions. Second, when the intrinsic quality of the product is known, consider how marketable it is. Remember that customers will not buy on taste. They will buy on the wine's brand image and any advice the staff can give before a choice is made.

Throughout this process restaurateurs must force themselves to refer their choices back into the context of the restaurant. They alone know what sort of customers they are aiming at and who they currently serve. The ultimate arbiter of a winelist is the customer. If they want to drink Piesporter or Clos de Vougeot every day then they must be satisfied.

QUESTIONS AND EXERCISES

1. Arrange a wine tasting for yourself and a few friends or colleagues. This need not be an expensive affair, a few reasonably priced and well chosen wines, a reasonably spacious room, some clean glasses and a note pad and pen for all those taking part. Various things to consider are

   - Taste the wines 'blind' – that is without knowing which wines you have tasted until *after* you have made your mind up about which ones you prefer and finished making you notes.
   - Make sure that the tasting has a 'theme' – it could be that you are tasting wines from the same region but from different producers, or the same grape but different countries.
   - Set yourself an objective. Imagine you are the manager of a restaurant and have to choose one of the wines in front of you – which one would it be?
   - Try making notes in different styles. For one tasting try making very comprehensive notes. For another simply use key words that remind you of which wine it was and your basic impression.

2. Make notes of *all* the wines you drink – even if just a few lines written after the event to remind you of the name and vintage and whether you thought the wine was good or not. A very good discipline to get into at an early stage is some sort of easy note retrieval system. Otherwise they can be very hard to access when they have grown to notes on thousands of wines.
3. Occasionally try to make notes (even mental ones) on everyday smells and tastes. Ultimately your notes on wine describe what it tastes 'like' and these 'like' items are drawn from everyday smell and tastes.
4. From your notes at a wine tasting write down various sample descriptions that you could use on a restaurant wine list.
5. As a spontaneous exercise write down the ten wines that first come to mind (try not to think about it too hard). When you have listed the wines ask various questions:

- Are these 'popular' wines?
- With time can you think of a less well known alternative? Does this offer better value for money/greater opportunity for bigger margins?
- With the help of a price list or wine guide find out if the wines you first listed command a premium price for their fame (if indeed you chose famous names).
- For each wine you have listed where you can find a better value alternative, develop a strategy for influencing consumers to buy the alternative instead of the more popular wine.

FURTHER READING.

There are two great works on the subject of wine tasting. The more accessible and perhaps the best for those who want a fully comprehensive introduction to the practicalities of wine tasting, is *Michael Broadbent's Pocket Guide to Winetasting*. This was first published as *Wine Tasting* in 1968 and has been revised and republished several times since. This book is now part of the excellent series of slimline wine and drink books published by Mitchell Beazley.

For those who want a more comprehensive and scientific approach, *The Taste of Wine* (Le Goût du Vin) by Emile Peynaud (1987) is, by any definition, comprehensive.

4 Purchasing wine

> **Key concepts**
>
> The main concepts covered in this chapter are:
> - supply structure;
> - supplier selection;
> - developing a supplier policy.

INTRODUCTION

The importance of the UK in the world wine trade is worth restating. The curious blend of history, trade agreements and invention that has stood the country so well in the past, continues to bear fruit right up to the present day. For the restaurateur though the country's history is of less importance than the very real benefits that its status confers within the world wine trade.

The most obvious benefit is the vast and varied ranges that are the hallmark of most reputable wine merchants. Unlike many nations which have domestic wine-producing industries to support, as merely a trader in wine the UK has no need for protectionist chauvinism. Although wines imported from within the European Union obtain some benefits over those from so-called 'Third Countries' (outside the EU), when the UK joined the EU the withdrawal of the Imperial Preference System brought an end to any favouritism in wine imports.

The second hallmark of many of the ranges in wine merchants' shops is the quality of the wine. Unlike many countries, particularly those close to the Mediterranean, the standard British thirst quenching drink has always been beer. Large quantities of cheap, unremarkable table wines have never been a feature of the British table in the way that they are in France, Spain or Italy.

For both these reasons and because many of the world's most respected and influential wine writers live in the UK, producers that wish to release a quality wine will try to gain an initial foothold in the UK, where success would result in the wine being viewed more favourably by other nations.

Such status inevitably has both benefits and drawbacks. Not only is the market filled with a vast number of high quality and extremely saleable wines, but many producers complain that it is also the most price sensitive. For example, when Spatz Sperling, vintner from Delheim wines, South Africa, was on a promotional visit to the UK he commented that he could almost name his price in most of the countries they supplied. But in Britain, he complained, everyone wanted wines for specific price points such as £4.90, £5.90, and so on. His margins were cut so tight that he wished he could forget about Britain, but as a market it was too important. For the restaurateur this means that wines bought from merchants, even with the punitive tax levels levied on alcohol in the UK, still represent good value for money. Unfortunately the customer has also become sophisticated and is very price sensitive with regard to wine, maintaining the pressure on margins right through the sales process.

SUPPLY STRUCTURE

Ordinary retail customers generally have a limited choice of outlets from which to buy wine – usually high street retail wine merchants. Auctions, En Primeur (a method of buying young fine wines before they are bottled or shipped), and mail order clubs all provide different opportunities, but mostly require substantial capital outlay or at least the purchase of a case. Restaurateurs, on the other hand, have far more variety of choice, ranging from the retailer/ wholesaler that gives more favourable terms for guaranteed regular business, through buying from a variety of middlemen and brokers, to buying from wine makers and taking the responsibility to ship and store it privately. The rest of this chapter considers how to make decisions about which level of this supply tree to buy from, and how to choose from the plethora of merchants and brokers at each level.

The traditional supply structure

It is worth describing briefly how hotels and restaurants used to buy their wines. Until recently this was usually a costly process that involved a very large capital outlay by hotel and restaurant proprietors for a product which was often not as good or unadulterated as the one enjoyed today. Typically, the growers harvested the grapes and then either vinified it (made it into wine) themselves or sold the grapes to a wine broker, known in France (the most common source of wine) as a *négociant-éleveur*. *Négociants* blended the wines of different growers together to produce a more harmonious and consistent product. This was followed by a period of 'élevage' (hence the term 'éleveur') or maturation prior to being sold.

At this stage, very large hotels would go to the *négociants* to buy wines direct. These would then be shipped back to their cellars (often on the premises) and gradually sold through the restaurant. The advantage of this system was that long-term supply was guaranteed. At a time when the integrity of suppliers could not always be relied upon, a certain degree of control was exercised over the wine. Adulteration of blended wines was until recently quite common, involving the mixing of wines from very hot climate countries to boost a blend of rather insipid wine from a poor vintage. Buying in great bulk, with only the grower and *négociant* previously involved, limited the opportunity for this sort of fraud to some degree.

However, there were obvious disadvantages to such a system. Massive funds were required to finance the purchase. The money used then lay tied up for months or even years while the stock was gradually sold through the restaurant.

The modern supply structure

The modern supply structure for wines is somewhat more complicated, requiring rather more effort on behalf of the commercial buyers in order to understand it. There are certainly far more ways of buying than through the traditional system. In the modern trade people at different levels of the chain of supply may well be keen to supply to restaurants or hotels, the defining factor usually being the volumes involved. Certainly those who wish to buy very large volumes of wine will find that they can buy from dealers in the producer country, if not from the producers themselves. Those who are buying smaller amounts will find that they are restricted to the different outlets for wholesale wine purchases in the UK.

The different agents, *négociants*, wholesalers, and others all link together in a variety of ways that can at first look incredibly complicated. They are all best described by their roles.

Producers

Producers are always the original source of at least the grapes from which wine is made. Some, like the huge Australian companies, own vast tracts of land which produce large quantities of wine, quite possibly with well-known brand names. These firms can incorporate the functions of other links in the supply chain by shipping and marketing their own wines and employing staff in the final destination countries to act as agents who will arrange to have it sold through various wholesale and retail outlets.

Alternatively, producers can be those who, by inheritance or deliberate purchase, own a small vineyard holding which produces a few grapes each year while they hold another job elsewhere. This is very much the situation in European countries such as France and particularly Germany. Often (though not always) these producers do not vinify their own wine but sell the grapes on to either another vigneron, *négociant* or co-operative. The grapes can then be made into wine, either to be bottled alone or to be blended with the produce of other small growers.

Between these two extremes there is a whole range of differently sized producers, with some of them combining the role of producer with *négociant* (or similar broker role if not in France) right through to the Australian example of dealing with almost every aspect of production and handling of their wines. The strength of the large co-operative producers lies in this system. By having a central facility for the vinification of grapes from all their members, they make access possible to the very latest hi-tech wine production methods for even the small growers. From there the wines can be tended by qualified oenologists and chemical analysts, as well as sold by skilled marketing teams.

For the restaurateur, there is often little scope for dealing direct with producers. Exceptions to this are those who need to satisfy a large demand for wine, have the capital to take fairly large amounts, and can afford to store it (often in a bonded warehouse, where alcohol can be stored without paying duty until it is released). This is the approach taken by outlets with a high wine turnover, particularly in house wines, ensuring that they have a continuous supply of these vital wines while they continue to use merchants and other wholesalers for the rest of their list.

Buying from producers direct in this way is something of a specialist skill and needs to be approached with caution. Problems that can face the intrepid buyer are currency market fluctuations, dealing with shippers and the legal requirements associated with importing alcohol into the UK. Given the complexity of the process, and the fact that the law relating to customs and excise issues in particular can change very quickly, it will not be discussed in any detail here, save to say that advice from experienced wine buyers and shipping companies is vital. Merchants are not necessarily the best sources of information since it is not in their interests to encourage 'cutting out the middleman' in this lucrative part of the business, but other restaurateurs and hoteliers can give invaluable guidance.

Agents

Agents are the representatives of a wine in the destination country. Almost all wines have agents who perform a range of tasks, from selling it to retailers by giving them samples and arranging marketing activities through to actually selling it direct (if they are retailers or wholesalers). Some firms work exclusively as agents to one particular firm of producers and may only have a limited number of wines on their books. These 'agencies' are often no more than one person with a fax and telephone operating from home, merely using the services of bonded warehouses, shippers and haulage firms to service their customers. Other agents will handle the wines of a number of producers and will have their own office and storage facilities and delivery capability.

This level of the business can provide a great deal for large restaurateurs and hoteliers who are seeking to buy reasonable quantities of wine and are prepared to deal with a variety of suppliers. Many British independent merchants buy the majority of their wine through agents so it is possible to see the quantities that are required. But some restaurants can move as much wine as a small merchant and there is no need for them to feel that they should be precluded from cutting out the middleman in the form of the merchant in this way. In seeking an agent it should be remembered that many agencies are not household names. It is therefore important to get hold of the wine trade reference, *Harper's Trade Directory*, and to find who is agent for what. Some specialize in specific regions or countries, also set out in the *Directory*.

WINE TRADE PERIODICALS

Given the influence that wine merchants can have over the wines served in restaurants, it can be interesting to find out rather more about them. One of the best sources of information is through the wine trade's own periodicals.

The wine trade is served by three different journals. For many, the voice of the wine trade is *Harper's*, a weekly paper (in magazine format) containing news, features, diary dates and jobs. Subscribers also receive the annual *Harper's Trade Directory*, almost a national Yellow Pages of wine trade companies at all levels, as well as firms such as analytical chemists, bottle manufacturers and bonded warehouses that serve the wine trade.

The competitor to *Harper's* is *Wine and Spirit International*. This rather larger publication is more comprehensive in its features, although occasionally this makes it less current. For those not directly involved in the day-to-day business of the wine trade this can be a more interesting read.

Finally, many wine merchants receive the weekly *Off-Licence News*. This contains information about executive changes, product news, 'advertorials', special features (often with a seasonal flavour), as well as competitions including the multi-category *Off-Licence of the Year*.

Having identified likely suppliers (and ensured that the quantities you require are large enough) they should be then approached for samples and details of prices and minimum case loads and discounts (see below). However, do not be surprised if after approaching an agent they refer you to another firm elsewhere. Some agencies make exclusive agreements or contracts with wholesalers to sell the wine only through them (there may be several covering different regions). This avoids the problems of actually providing a final outlet for the wine or physically having to deal with it.

The disadvantages of dealing with agencies are several. Few agencies have a great number of different brands. Unless they incorporate another role, perhaps as a specialist importer and wholesaler, they will rarely be able to provide wines for a full list or even the majority of it. They are also quantity sellers. The savings that can be made by going direct to an agent are there precisely because of the quantities involved. Any prospective buyer must be sure that they can justify (and afford) to buy whatever wines they supply in large numbers of cases.

Wholesalers

For commercial buyers wholesale merchants are the final chain in the wine trade hierarchy. They cover a multitude of outlets. At their most simple they can be retail outlets that produce a wholesale list as an adjunct to their core retail business. This may well be accompanied by account facilities and a delivery service. Alternatively they may be principally wholesalers who also sell retail as a sideline. Since high street premises are by no means necessary (or even desirable for many), these businesses often operate out of industrial estates or business parks. As pointed out above, many of the wines are bought through British-based agents, although fast moving, bulk lines are often bought direct. The main method of selling to hotels and restaurants is through sales teams on the road.

For most restaurants wholesalers are the principal source of wine, allowing purchases to be made in much smaller quantities and from a considerably larger range than could be provided by an agent. Wholesalers may offer other advantages such as account facilities, wine list production services and frequent deliveries. They often also sell glassware, bar equipment and other sundry items. Their main task is to convince restaurateurs to take more wines from them as opposed to rival merchants and hopefully to monopolize the whole list.

SUPPLIER SELECTION

From this very much simplified description of the wine trade it is possible to see that it consists of a complicated system of producers, brokers and other dealers who trade in wine, all variously interlinked depending on their size and the quantities involved. However, the basic rule is the same as that for many traded commodities. For small quantities, a greater level of service and ease of purchase it is always best to go to the bottom of the pyramid. But if restaurateurs are in the position to buy a large quantity and have the time, experience and confidence to take on a greater responsibility for the wine or to deal with a multiplicity of different agents, then they may find that they can realize genuine savings.

In deciding what approach to take it is worth considering a few questions about the style of outlet involved and what is required from a merchant, at whatever level in the supply structure in the trade. Such an approach can help very small restaurateurs to decide between the merits of various local wholesalers, as well as help a very large restaurant decide on major questions such as whether to ship their own house wine.

Predicting volumes

The first question in any decision about where to buy wine from is what volumes are involved. This is followed by what are the requirements of the outlet. If the restaurant is just starting up, initial business plans will be the source of this sort of information. At this level it is best to play safe and purchase wine from wholesale merchants, adopting a policy of forgoing any possible financial benefits gained from buying in great volume in favour of the peace of mind of having a simple list that does not tie up cash in stock but leaves it free to develop the business.

For more established outlets the questions become more complex. Day-to-day planning is done at its most basic on a system of refilling bin spaces in the cellar and keeping set numbers of cases of house wines. The basis for ordering is then refined by the use of historic records or order books. These show patterns of sales and when to increase ordering of lines that have a seasonal or special influence such as Valentine's Day, bank holidays or prebooked birthday parties. This subject is developed in more detail in Chapter 5 – Beverage Control.

For those who wish to ship their own wine, accurate volume prediction becomes essential. Shippers look to deliver in loads of fifty or more, and the lead times on deliveries (the time between ordering and delivery) can be several weeks. Errors made here can mean that the restaurant goes without wine for a fortnight, or ends up with cash tied up unnecessarily in excess stock. If a restaurant is going to embark on this sort of procedure then it must be done cautiously, with records of volumes that can be trusted and a very healthy cash flow.

One supplier or many

Received hotel wisdom holds that it is foolhardy for any manager to use only one supplier for the wine list. The reasoning behind this is that it is foolhardy to put too much faith in any one supplier, particularly when the commodity is something as important as the restaurant's wine. For instance, it is easy to imagine the havoc that would be caused if the sole supplier was unable to deliver prior to a bank holiday, or through its own fault ran out of house wines and was unable to supply them for a fortnight. If an outlet is served by a variety of merchants, one of the others may well be able to maintain a reasonable selection in the interim.

The second problem with being exclusively served by a single supplier is that all the restaurant lists in an area will begin to look remarkably similar. These problems become compounded if one company dominates the region and restaurant diners begin to notice the similarity of all the lists. So again, if the wine list is made up of a variety of wines from a variety of merchants, the variation will leave it looking individual and different from local competitors.

However, there are reasons for buying from a single wine merchant, at the simplest those of necessity. In more remote parts of the UK there may be only one merchant who can supply restaurants – unless restaurateurs are prepared to make large capital outlays on wine which is subsequently stored at their expense until the firm is able to deliver again. Alternatively, there are restaurants that operate in concert with or as part of a wine merchant's business. These restaurants, although they may well be highly reputable in their own right, act as a valuable showcase for the wine merchant.

For most restaurants though, wine merchants are like any other supplier. They exist to provide a commodity on which restaurateurs make their money. Therefore it may be advisable to build up a rapport with merchants in order to secure better terms in the future. Some restaurants are prepared to risk the 'eggs in one basket' scenario in favour of a wine company that will deliver out of hours or at short notice in recognition of valuable custom. Certainly it is not hard to imagine a situation where a customer buys all the stock of one superb wine on a Friday. The restaurant loses the chance of selling it again on a Saturday and has to disappoint customers in the process because the merchant has no Saturday delivery facility. Instead it could be worth giving all the wine list to a single firm that will ensure Saturday delivery under any circumstances.

The second point to consider is the administrative difficulty of keeping track of the wines from perhaps half a dozen suppliers. Many wine merchants have encountered the problem of restaurants ordering a long list of wines, only to discover that several of them are not theirs. This situation arises when the staff given the task of ordering the wines were not involved in the original selection of the list. If the list is built up of the wines of a number of suppliers, the ordering procedure must take this into account, with a master list clearly telling the staff what comes from where. The ordering procedure must also record the fact that many suppliers have a minimum delivery of one or two cases (12 or 24 bottles). A frequent scenario is where the restaurant is desperate for one wine from a particular supplier but is unable to find enough quantity to make up the order. In this situation, if all the wine comes from a single supplier there will usually be a requirement for house wine that will bulk out the order.

Finally, small restaurants or those just starting up are rarely best served by developing a complicated list filled with the wines of a variety of suppliers. Simplicity is vital. Build up a relationship with one supplier that can then help when developing a more complex list. This also gives the restaurateur more power when negotiating for better deals later on. A wine merchant that is afraid to lose a loyal customer is more likely to give a special price on perhaps a staple house wine. Alternatively they may buy in something specially (particularly if they feel they have a guaranteed outlet) or give a generous allocation of a restricted supply wine to their most faithful customers.

The range of merchant services

Wine merchants may be prepared to offer better terms if they have an exclusive deal on the wines for a restaurant. However, it is vital that any restaurateur takes an objective look at the range of services of all the local merchants, including what they would offer for exclusivity. The relatively low mark-ups that most wine merchants can command on their wines and the competitive nature of the trade mean that on the whole they are best distinguished by the services they offer, and not on the basis of price alone. It is rare if not impossible to find two lists of apparently comparable wines where one provides considerably better value that the other. Good quality wines cost about the same, no matter who offers them. The best way to distinguish merchants is on the basis of what fringe benefits they offer the customer.

Bulk discounts

Discounts are the first and most obvious place to look for value from a wine merchant. They need not exist across the whole range of wines, but if a restaurant expects to sell a great deal of house wine or is prepared to take much larger deliveries less frequently, then it is worth asking whether better terms can be offered. Alternatively, restaurateurs who own or buy wine for more than one outlet can enquire whether better terms could be given if the basic house wines in the two restaurants were the same. Some merchants also give small extra discounts for cash or immediate payment. Being prepared always to collect your own wines instead of requiring delivery may also reduce the price a little. Thus, instead of simply accepting a blanket set of terms, set out what is required in the way of service. By making the wine merchant's life easier, find out if they would be prepared to give better discounts.

Credit

Most wine merchants offer some sort of credit facility for restaurants. This enables the restaurateurs to sell some or all of the wine before it has even been paid for, while the merchants do not have to worry about collection of payment on their rounds. The usual period of credit is one month, but it may be worth finding out whether this could be extended occasionally and what the exact terms of credit are. Again it is worth reiterating that if restaurants are prepared to pay for their goods on receipt, merchants often give better terms than their list price.

Delivery

When asking a wine merchant about delivery the main areas of concern for the restaurateur are how often, when, at what cost, and in what quantity? The first question, how often, is perhaps the most important. For most restaurants weekly delivery is an absolute minimum. Many require deliveries far more frequently, not least to deal with the unpredictable nature of wine sales which can easily leave a restaurant out of stock of a particular wine very quickly.

The timing of restaurant deliveries can also be critical and should not coincide with the height of lunchtime, or when everyone is trying to get a rest during the afternoon. The day of the week is also of concern and must take into account when the outlet is closed and when it is most convenient for the restaurateur.

The final questions of at what cost and in what quantity are vitally important for small outlets. All good merchants will offer a free delivery service, and the best will deliver even a single bottle to a regular customer. Some though will charge for deliveries smaller than say three or four cases, and/or only accept orders for a case or more. This can be a deciding factor for small country hotels and guest houses where stock levels are very low. It can also be important for larger units where there is the occasional need for 'emergency' deliveries at critical times. There are occasions when it is easy to forgive a great many faults in the wine merchant that is prepared to come out on a Saturday or bank holiday to make an extra delivery in its own time.

Other services

Here wine merchants can really distinguish themselves from the opposition by offering services that make a restaurateur's life much easier. One simple way is to provide wine glasses and other equipment such as measures, decanters and ice buckets.

Some merchants will draw up wine lists and have them printed and bound for the restaurant. As the merchants know the wines most intimately they can usually be relied upon to describe them correctly and even put in points of interest (if this is the style of list required). Help in marketing wines in other ways – suggesting wines of the month, making up tent cards for tables – can all provide extra profit, come free from the merchant and are worth pursuing. Some merchants can also be persuaded to give their time for tastings, although bear in mind several points before asking them to do this. Wine merchants are continually asked to give tastings. Although they may be marvellous fun for the audience and even the hosts, they require a major effort on the part of the merchants. Time has to be spent drawing up what they will say, an evening has to be given up – and all for free. This can be particularly galling when celebrities from the wine world command fees of over £1,500 for a single appearance. Tastings will always be arranged for genuine and proven long-term customers and when the merchant can see some real commercial benefit at the end of it. However, for the most part merchants are weary of turning down requests from complete strangers and those looking for a free chance to bring custom into the restaurant.

DEVELOPING A SUPPLIER POLICY

There is evidently more to choosing a merchant than simply going to the person with the nicest looking wine list. Shrewd restaurateurs will take all the above factors into consideration and apply them to their own circumstances. First, they must consider their own position, primarily how much they want to buy. Second, how much effort and time can they give to the maintenance of their wine list? Can they be bothered to deal with a multiplicity of merchants? What sort of deliveries do they require? How do they intend to pay? By credit or cash? Only when the restaurateurs are quite sure what they want should they approach wine merchants, which should be assessed in the light of what the restaurateurs know they want. Then by negotiation a deal should be struck that provides the best value for the restaurant.

However, the owners of a small country restaurant are not well served by dealing with a large national company if they have to struggle to order a case and cannot call in to collect half a dozen bottles of house wine on a bank holiday. Equally, large hotels will not be satisfied by a single small merchant which cannot keep up with their demand for house wine and effectively charges them a handling charge for wines they could easily ship themselves. The small restaurant deals best with the single merchant that gives marketing advice, drops in small deliveries on the way home, and allows extended credit when cash flow becomes a bit tight. As for the big hotels, why should they spend money on jobs they could do themselves, or run the risk of being let down by a single supplier? Their buying power is best put to use in volume purchasing that guarantees regular supply (there is nothing more regular than having it on the premises) and eliminates payment for services they can do themselves.

QUESTIONS AND EXERCISES

1. For the following types of restaurant, develop a wine supplier strategy by identifying what their particular needs are, what sort of wine list they are likely to have and what sort of services you feel they are likely to require:

   - a countryside guest house, offering home cooked meals to its residents, a largely seasonal mix of walkers and older domestic tourists on a short break with their car;
   - a fashionable brasserie in a city centre location, popular with office workers and evening diners;
   - an independently managed country pub trying to move away from traditional pub fare to a more adventurous menu and wine list;
   - the student training restaurant in a university/college.

2. Either as a group or individually get in touch with two or three wine merchants and find out what services they are prepared to offer business clients. Compare what different merchants have to offer and how flexible they would be in meeting the needs of various types of restaurant.

3. 'Restaurants who buy their wine through merchants are needlessly paying middlemen who serve no other purpose than to provide expensive wine storage facilities.' Is this ever the case?

4. One supplier suggests that they can give a complete package, all your wines, good discounts, delivery, a wine list service, friendly advice – if you like a 'one-stop shop'. Explain why this is not necessarily a good idea and you should use a variety of suppliers.

5. Write the introduction to a wine merchant's brochure that explains why this particular wine merchant is an especially wise choice for restaurateurs wanting to buy wine for their outlet.

FURTHER READING

For historical reading on the history of the wine trade, a number of wine history books cover the development of the trade, for instance, *The Story of Wine* by Hugh Johnson (1989) and *Wine and the Vine* by Tim Unwin (1991). However a more specific text is *Anatomy of the Wine Trade* by Simon Loftus (1985).

More recently two books by Andrew Barr have concentrated to a degree on the wine trade both in the UK and abroad. *Wine Snobbery* (1988), described as an 'insiders guide to the booze business', is a fascinating insight into some of the less savoury facts of the wine trade. The more recent *Drink* (1995), 'an informal social history', looked at a far wider range of drinks than simply wine but contains some interesting details on the development of the wine trade in the UK.

For those who want information on the current UK wine trade, the two trade journals, *Harpers* and *Wine and Spirit International*, are the best sources of reference.

5 Beverage control

> **Key concepts**
>
> The main concepts covered in this chapter are:
>
> - issues in berverage control;
> - wine stock control systems;
> - performance measures;
> - wine pricing.

INTRODUCTION

Anyone involved in or studying hospitality management needs an awareness of at least the basics of stock control. Hospitality units make purchases of food and drink as well as sundry items from a variety of suppliers and need to have an accurate picture of stock levels at all times.

Various factors within the hospitality industry give stock control especial importance. Of particular interest here is what has been termed the 'Culture of Informal Rewards' (for instance, Wood, 1994:10) that runs throughout the industry. As basic pay is often poor, staff are tempted to supplement their wages by pilfering from stock, either to consume themselves or in order to sell on. While not condoned this is often seen as part of general industry practice, engendering a culture of acceptance among management which allows pilferage to flourish.

A second factor, which has particular relevance to this book, is that beverage stocks are relatively simple items to steal. For those drinks that are sold by the measure (and with sales of wine by the glass, wine can be included) lost quantity can be made up by adding either inferior liquor or water. For those drinks that are sold unopened, their containers (think, for example, of a wine bottle) are made to be easily portable. Managers cannot watch all their staff all the time, indeed such an atmosphere of distrust is only likely to encourage staff to see the company as 'fair game' when it comes to pilferage. Furthermore, as a luxury product alcoholic beverages are particularly desirable items to steal.

Third, notwithstanding the loss to operators in the cost of pilfered drink, the high mark-up of wines in particular means that this represents a significant loss of revenue potential

Unfortunately worries about theft and pilferage sometimes occupy managers to the extent that they ignore other facets of beverage control. Wines and spirits are such high mark-up items that it is possible for them to contribute a very large amount of the final profit to a restaurant. Thus, if they are badly chosen and not managed carefully their poor delivery can have an effect on the performance of the whole restaurant. To get the sort of information required properly to manage wines and spirits needs careful beverage control that yields important information about the performance of different drinks. From this information those wines or other drinks that fail to perform can be phased out and those that are popular money-spinners promoted.

The second part of this chapter is devoted to the question of wine pricing. This is a difficult area as it is often a subject of contention between restaurateur and customer. Many customers perceive restaurant wine lists as being prohibitively expensive. While some restaurateurs make attempts to have wine lists as reasonable as possible, they face the problem that they are not able to make a realistic profit from their operations, with wine appearing to be the easiest target for price increases. Unfortunately for those who do work hard to make wines sell reasonably, they too face consumer criticism. Consumers frequently compare prices, not with other restaurants, but with high street wine retailers, with whom restaurateurs have no hope of competing.

The pricing section gives some ways of getting around these thorny problems, as well as considering the mechanics of pricing wines and what sort of pricing policy should apply in different styles of outlet.

ISSUES IN BEVERAGE CONTROL

On the whole beverage control is far simpler than food control. The number of different products to keep track of is far smaller, and they come from fewer suppliers. When they do arrive they are in known and easily identifiable amounts and of a known quality. Finally beverages, particularly wines and spirits have much longer shelf lives. The following issues must be kept in mind when establishing stock control procedures to ensure that primarily the customer is always satisfied, and that it is done to ensure the maximum profitability for the restaurant.

Choice

Understandably, customers find it incredibly irritating when they have made a choice of wine only to find that it is not available. This is particularly infuriating if the wine was to go with specific choices from the menu. A control system should incorporate not only routine reordering to ensure consistent supply, but also allow for changes in anticipated demand when the menu is changed, which will alter the wines favoured. For instance, if a restaurant were to feature a special game promotion (grouse, venison and hare) rather than a routine reordering of wines sold in the previous purchasing period, the next order should anticipate demand during the promotion for full-bodied reds that go particularly well with game.

Cost

The importance of wine cost can be illustrated with a very basic example. Take a small restaurant with twenty-four wines on its list, carrying five bottles of each wine at an average cost of £5 a bottle. The cost of those wines is £600. Now if the restaurant were for some reason to carry one bottle more of each wine unnecessarily, the cost increases £720. Of the restaurant's capital £120 is tied up needlessly when it could be doing something useful such as buying furniture, other forms of stock or simply reducing any bank loans. Thus, when establishing stock levels there has to be a careful balance between the cost of extra stock and the possibility of having too little stock to satisfy customers.

Suppliers

When considering the choice of supplier the situation of the restaurant must be considered. There are restaurants positioned literally next door to their suppliers. These can adopt a more flexible approach to ordering as staff are able simply to walk in and buy a bottle if they run out. Alternatively there are those who by choice or necessity buy wine from merchants many miles away that are perhaps only able to deliver infrequently. These considerations will have a major impact on the systems and the levels of stock carried.

Vulnerability of wine

Wine is vulnerable from a variety of sources. Although wines have a much greater shelf life than food stocks and, for instance, keg beers, they can suffer degradation from storage conditions. Wine suffers when it is exposed to too much light which is counteracted to some degree by using coloured glass in bottles. However, most bottle colours are inefficient at filtering out ultraviolet radiation, the harmful part of the light entering the bottle. Tradition and brand image probably best explain why producers are reluctant to change bottle style and colour as the change would confuse customers (Jackson, 1994: 322). Ironically, white wines, which appear to suffer most light damage (Macpherson, 1982, cited in Jackson, ibid.) are often those in the lightest coloured bottles, possibly to make it easier for consumers to identify the colour of the wine.

Second, wine is vulnerable to heat damage, particularly if this is associated with long periods of exposure to sunlight. As the ageing of wine is a chemical process, the temperature at which wine is stored has a direct effect on the speed of the various reactions taking place (Jackson, 1994: 330). Common symptoms of heat degradation are a loss of aroma and fruit as aromatic compounds like esters and terpenes disappear. Sometimes wines develop a 'baked' smell from reactions involving the wine's sugars. Heat degradation can also lead to a browning of the wine's colour, and in red wines a sediment may form. Finally, increased heat or even a varying temperature affect the volume of wine in the bottle and can loosen the cork. This lets wine seep out and bacteria seep in. Noticeable changes in heat-affected wine can take place within even a few days. Therefore it is very important to ensure that when stock is bought it is handled with care and that only suitable places are used to store wine, not just every available space. Equally, restaurateurs should try wines periodically to ensure that they are not being given wines that have suffered this sort of degradation during transport or at their merchant's premises.

Third, there is the problem of vulnerability from theft. It is worth remembering that smaller stocks are often more manageable and that watertight stock control systems will act as a deterrent, as well as promptly highlighting any problem areas.

WINE STOCK CONTROL SYSTEMS

Stock control systems cover a large area and have a number of textbooks devoted to them. At their heart they are relatively simple, working on the principle that all stock should be traceable back to its source. If there is a discrepancy, it should be obvious from the paperwork where this has occurred. Clearly this is the ideal situation and few outlets could claim to have a completely watertight method, but the development of any stock control system should try to stick to this logic.

Procedures used by different outlets vary according to the size of unit, with larger units requiring more complex systems. But these complex systems are ultimately extensions of a simple procedure familiar to the managers of the smallest units. For the purposes of this book a description of this simplified procedure is adequate. The control systems used by the very largest hotel and restaurant groups are specific to those groups and describing them in detail would be rather pointless. Second, wine stock control in larger units is simply a small part of much larger food and beverage control systems incorporating spirits, beers and soft drinks which are beyond the scope of this book.

Goods received

From the moment that wines are carried through the door there should be a record of them which can be matched against a delivery note and any subsequent invoice. Wine merchants experience many different requests with regard to delivery notes, with some units being keener to check all the items delivered than others. Equally, some units prefer to be given priced delivery notes, while others prefer unpriced delivery notes to keep their mark-up levels secret even from staff (reducing the temptation for staff to help themselves). Either way the delivery note should record clearly the wines being delivered and the number of each. When this has been checked and found to be correct, both the copies (one for the restaurant, one proof of delivery for the wine merchant) should be signed. All the products are then entered into a Goods Received Book. Essentially this records the following:

- date and time;
- name (and address) of the supplier;
- delivery note number and/or invoice number;
- description of wines delivered;
- quantity of each wine;
- signature or initials of whoever enters the details.

There are obvious variations on this procedure. For instance, there are control systems, often in larger units, that work not on bottle numbers but on the cost of items passing through the system or their potential revenue. In this case the cost of wines also needs to be entered into the Goods Received Book. Equally, for some very small restaurants the numbers involved are so small and deliveries so infrequent that rather than record them in a Goods Received Book and then transfer them to a Cellar Stock Ledger (see below) they can simply be recorded directly onto the Cellar Stock Card.

Cellar stock ledger and bin cards

Within the cellar each wine is recorded in two ways. All wines should have separately identifiable bin spaces. Each bin space should have its own bin card, recording the time and volume of movements in and out of stock of each wine and the current balance, which must agree with the stock in the bin. These cards can also show other information such as the maximum stock level (either the maximum bin capacity or the predetermined affordable level). Alternatively they can show the minimum stock level to alert staff that the wine needs reordering.

Second, the Cellar Stock Ledger records all movements into and out of the cellar. This Ledger shows stock movements in rather more detail than the bin cards, showing where the wine originated from and where it has been sent. The detail will show what wine was moved, its cost price and who authorized the movement.

Wine requisitions

No wine should leave the cellar without a proper requisition procedure, again continuing the chain so that all movements can be traced back to the beginning. A numbered duplicate or triplicate book is the most common way of ensuring that this continuity is maintained. Requisition notes need to make clear what is required, how much and for which department. They also need to have the date and the signature of the person authorizing the transfer. The system itself varies but is commonly:

- the top copy in the cellar, its serial number recorded in the Cellar Stock Ledger and kept there;
- the duplicate copy goes to whoever is responsible for stock control. In large units this is a separate department, but in small units it allows the manager to keep a separate record of stock movements;

- the triplicate copy acts like a delivery note, allowing the receiving department to check that they received the stock they asked for.

The amount that is reordered each day should conform to a set procedure, usually bringing stock levels up to par stock. This avoids overstocking in any one department, and unnecessary reordering. Par stock is at its simplest the maximum the department might require, plus a small safety margin. Requisition is then a question of bringing stock up to par every day.

There is an alternative method of determining par stock (Durkan and Cousins, 1995: 123), particularly if there is a large number of wines to keep track of. This also uses past sales data, although in a rather more rigid formula:

$$M = W(T+L)+S$$

where

M = Maximum stock
W = Average usage rate
T = Review period
L = Lead time
S = Safety stock (buffer or minimum)

An example of using this formula could be:

W = 24 bottles per week
T = 4 weeks
L = 1 week
S = 1 week's usage (i.e. 24 bottles)
$M = 24(4+1)+24 = 144$ bottles

Minimum stock (buffer or safety stock) may be calculated as follows:

$L \times W = 1 \times 24 = 24$ bottles

ROL (re-order level) may be calculated as follows:

$(W \times L)+S = (24 \times 1)+24 = 48$ bottles

This formula, and indeed the concept of par stock should be applied to all departments including the cellar, the only difference there being that the cellar must use its suppliers to restore its stock levels. In some small restaurants it is unnecessary to go to the lengths outlined above for each department (bar, restaurant, kitchen), but the formula can still be applied to the restaurant as a whole by simply taking into account stocks held in various locations.

Within the cellar as the stock is issued to the requisitioning department, the cellar's records must be updated, the bin card showing stock issued and adjusting the balance. The move is then recorded in the Cellar Stock Ledger.

Bar and sommelier records

Within the dispensing bar and restaurant the wines sold must be recorded so that sales can be cross checked and stock levels maintained. At the end of each day, the bar manager/sommelier using the retained top copy of any wine order checks, fills out a Daily Consumption Sheet showing how many bottles of each wine have been sold each day. At the end of each day or week this information is transferred to a Stock Book so that the amount needed to restore stock levels is worked out. This Stock Book also shows the cost (and/or potential revenue) of each product consumed in the period, which can be compared to the actual revenue generated through the till.

Wine ordering procedure

This brings the system round full circle. After making requisitions the various departments gradually deplete the cellar of its stocks of various wines, bringing them down to or below the predetermined re-order levels. The cellarman then writes out an official order, either in duplicate or triplicate, in both cases sending the top copy to the supplier. Writing out an order in this way is important, even if the wine is ordered over the telephone, as it keeps a vital record of what was ordered in case it is incorrect when it arrives. The bottom copy in both cases remains in the order book, and in the case of triplicate books the middle copy is sent to the accounts department. This is really only necessary in large outlets.

When the wines arrive the delivery note can be checked against the order recorded in the order book to ensure that the correct wines have been delivered. The wines and quantities can then be entered onto the relevant bin cards and Cellar Ledger Book and the control system reaches full circle.

Other stock control procedures

There is a number of other procedures that are used in ensuring good wine stock control. Some of these are vital to all outlets, some are dependent on the restaurant.

- **Transfer Book**. If wine is sent from one department to another this records those movements as well as the date and the signature of the person authorizing it. This is most common in restaurants with several bars or where the kitchen requisitions wine from a bar rather than from the cellar.
- **Ullage Book**. This keeps a record of all breakages so that they can then be accounted for as they will not appear on any sales checks. The cost of these wines will then come off the gross profit. In some cases it is useful to keep this book with a box to contain part of the bottle (usually the neck with the cork still in) to prove that the bottles genuinely were broken. These can then be checked occasionally by a manager against what is claimed in the book. The book should record the wine, the date, who broke it and who checked it off.
- **Returns**. All restaurants occasionally have bottles returned by customers. The way of dealing with this is covered in Chapter 8, but it can often lead to the wine going back to the merchant for a credit. Again this book should have a box for the wines to go in to be checked off. If returning wines, do not throw the wine away and do try to get the bottle to the merchant as quickly as possible to avoid any natural degradation of the wine.

- **Off-Sales Book**. This records the wines sold to customers for consumption off the premises (so long as the restaurant's licence allows for this). Any difference in price between that listed and that charged must be listed in this book, to be allowed against gross profit.
- **Staff Sales Book**. It is often in the restaurant's best interest to sell the staff wine either at cost or close to it. This means that they are well qualified to advised customers about wines, having had direct experience of them. While it is feasible to record these in the separate Off-Sales Book, if better terms are offered to the staff it is advisable to record them in a separate book.

PERFORMANCE MEASURES

Measuring the performance of a wine list is hampered in many restaurants by two factors. The first is a lack of available information, with many restaurants failing to keep adequate records of the performance of individual wines. The sort of information required is not only the number of bottles sold over a given period, but also the price and gross profit of a bottle, the time of day and time during the week when it sells best.

The second problem is that some restaurateurs judge a winelist on the same criteria as their wine loving customers. A list that contains the classic names of Burgundy and Bordeaux along with a few great Italian wines is often favoured over one with a good selection of German medium white wines and provincial French reds. Yet the first list is unlikely to have much under £20 and even at this price the gross profit is cut to the bone to sell bottles and customers often limit themselves to one bottle. The second list may well do far more to contribute to a healthy bottom line and thus in business terms be a 'better list'.

Grid group analysis

One tool that can help managers to decide if they should continue with wines or whether to change their list substantially is to use Grid Group Analysis (see Figure 5.1). The two axes of the grid show (A) the gross profit contribution and (B) the number of sales in a period. From this, wines are divided into four groups. The most productive wines are those that combine high sales with a high return and will appear in the top righthand quadrant of the graph. Those that do the opposite, combining low sales with a low margin are on the opposite

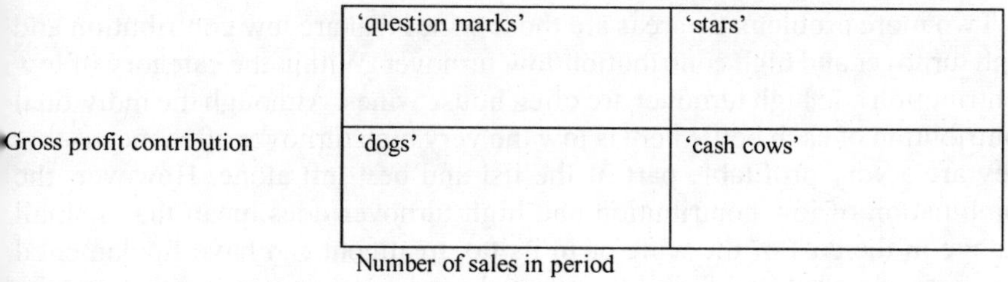

	'question marks'	'stars'
Gross profit contribution	'dogs'	'cash cows'

Number of sales in period

Figure 5.1 Grid Group Analysis.

side of the graph, the bottom lefthand side. The other two groups, high sales/low margin and low margin/high sales wines are in the bottom right and top left sides of the graph.

Maximizing wine profitability

A wine list where all the wines appear in the top right of a Grid Group Analysis graph could be described as the restaurateur's Holy Grail. Unfortunately, it is likely to remain as elusive as the Holy Grail while the wine market becomes more competitive and sophisticated and wine consumers become greater connoisseurs.

The restaurateur can do a great deal to maximize the list's profitability simply by acting on the results of Grid Group Analysis of a wine list. Those wines that are performing well, contributing a high margin and good sales, are the obvious candidates for any sort of sales promotion. Chapter 7 deals in detail with wine merchandizing and many of the techniques offered there can and should be applied to these profitable wines. At the heart of all of them is the desire to make consumers choose these wines over all the others.

There are three basic devices to make the customer choose these wines. First, there are blackboards, tent cards and wine list inserts that prompt undecided customers into buying a bottle by featuring the wine prominently. Second, there are devices such as special offers and good staff selling technique that urges a customer to buy a second or third bottle. Finally, there is the good selling technique of staff (and sometimes carefully scripted boards or winelists) that make customers who would normally choose a less profitable wine switch sale and go for the more profitable one.

Of the wines that appear in the bottom left of the graph, those that contribute the least and are rarely sold, the main question is whether to delist them. Maximizing profitability is not merely a question of increasing sales of the best wines, but minimizing the lost profitability of the least sold wines. Those wines that lie around the cellar are perceived by some restaurateurs as benign list fillers which are no cause for concern. In truth they are using up money that could be better spent on more profitable wines or even left in the bank and should be removed as soon as possible. In some very small outlets exceptions to this rule are when they are enjoyed by a few very loyal customers who would be upset if the wines were removed. Even so every effort should be made to convince the customers to change wines or to seek a more profitable alternative from a merchant.

Two more problematic areas are those wines that are low contribution and high turnover and high contribution/low turnover. Within the category of low contribution and high turnover are often house wines. Although the individual contribution of each bottle here is low the very high turnover often means that they are a very profitable part of the list and best left alone. However, the combination of low contribution and high turnover does mean that a small change in the cost of the wine or in its tax treatment can have fundamental ramifications on its profitability, seriously reducing or even wiping out the small margin. Thus, these wines require careful management and some effort in striking the best deal with a wine merchant. More borderline cases, those wines with a moderately high turnover and a low contribution, may require rather more action. It is worth considering whether to increase the price of the wine a little and what sort of consequences this would have on its turnover. For many wines that are sold on their names, the classic names of France and Germany and well-known producers from the New World, this is perfectly feasible. In deciding how far to push up the price, compare the prices of rival outlets for similar wines. Alternatively consider increasing the contribution in another way by looking for lower cost alternatives from other merchants.

The other category of high contribution/low margin wines contains two types of product. Those prestige products whose 'window dressing' qualities make up for their low turnover are dealt with below. The others are those which should be priced more effectively to increase turnover. Again, as for the wines described above, research the prices asked by competitors to find a price that will increase turnover. If reducing the price of any wine in this way do not waste the opportunity to make the most of the price change, by using boards or tent cards on tables and highlighting the change in the list, as well as instructing the staff to make the most of this selling opportunity.

Prestige wines and window dressing

Although not exclusively, the wines that represent high contribution/low turnover are prestigious and famous names from the best vintages. When customers see such names they will often remark on how good the list is, while choosing something cheaper and less well known. These wines are bought as a special treat, as part of a celebration or on expense accounts. The restaurateur should put them onto the list with some caution and with good advice. If they have a particularly low turnover there is the possibility that an odd bottle will lie untouched for such a long time that it will go past its best. Furthermore, even if the wines do eventually get sold there is the worry that the margin has long ago been eaten up by the cost of keeping them stored and taking up valuable space.

In choosing prestigious wines for the list ensure that they do have a reasonable chance of being sold, and within a reasonable timeframe. Check whether the merchant who sells them is prepared to take them back after a given period and replace them with an equivalent new vintage or different wine. Also consider the restaurant's own constraints.

- Are the storage facilities up to standard for such a delicate product?
- Can the staff sell it effectively?
- Does it tie in with the restaurant's image?
- Would the menu do justice to such a prestigious product?

If for some reason the wines are ruined their high cost has to come out of gross profit costing the restaurant a great deal for the sake of a relatively inefficient product.

WINE PRICING

Given the fact that so much resentment is levelled at restaurants for their high wine prices, not to mention the fact that wine is such a contributor to gross profit, wine pricing is given scant attention by many restaurateurs as well as by many textbooks. Consideration of wine pricing is far more than simply a case of dealing with the practical elements of how much to charge the customer for the product. A pricing policy can be used to make the integration of new and occasional products into the list far easier as well as help to market the restaurant. Increasingly, restaurateurs use their wine prices as a way of appealing to customers rather than leaving the wine list as secondary to the menu.

Methods of pricing

This is not a textbook on the detail of hospitality financial policy. Certainly, in larger outlets the mechanics of pricing wine will be part of a complex, integrated policy outside the scope of this book. However, these policies will adopt elements of the two basic methods of pricing.

- **Cost plus pricing**. This is perhaps the most traditional method and involves using the original cost of the product plus a percentage margin to establish the final price. In restaurant wine sales it has been very much the case that certain set percentages were used throughout the industry. In the 1950s restaurant mark-ups were about 200%. This was partly in response to a hangover from the days when restaurants imported their own wine from source and had to cover the extra cost of the capital outlay involved in the process. Today the generally accepted level is around 100 to 120%. On the whole the restaurateur wants the gross profit of a bottle to be around 60% of the original cost.

  The benefits of this system are that it is easy to implement and understand. Once the desired mark-up is known it is simply a question of going through the list adding on the percentage and VAT.

- **Market orientated pricing**. At the beginning of the wine boom in the 1950s and 1960s a system of rigid percentage margins was acceptable insofar as the customer knew no better. Nowadays the modern, sophisticated wine consumer must be treated with rather more respect and sensitivity. At the very least the cost plus method must be adapted to account for the prices of similar wines charged in rival outlets.

The nature of the product itself can lead to a far more sophisticated price treatment of each wine. As indicated before, easily recognized names from the classic regions of Europe can often sustain higher prices than lesser known wines of a similar quality. A very good example of this has been the treatment of Chablis, the Chardonnay wine from the north of Burgundy. Although prices reached astronomic and quite unreasonable levels in the 1980s many consumers were still happy to pay for it, as it was an easily recognizable wine, fashionable and with a distinguished history. Although it has recently seen its value fall rather more into line with other wines, it still commands a premium over and above a comparable Chardonnay from Australia or a lesser European region.

This concept is technically referred to as 'elasticity of demand' and is very useful in the pricing of wines. Those that are either famous like Chablis, or expensive (or both) are usually relatively elastic. That is to say adjustments in their price have little effect on the demand for them. This is particularly true of those that are more expensive, in that few people are going to notice a pound or two on a wine costing thirty. The converse of elastic wines are inelastic wines, the most important in this context being house wines. These are often priced very competitively to encourage customers to buy more bottles. However a pound on a bottle here with a bottle at under ten pounds can have disastrous consequences on sales.

Developing a pricing policy

For most restaurants the question of how to price wines is not so much a matter of choosing one method or another but of using a combination of the two. The method of pricing must also take into account the financial objectives of the business so that the eventual pricing policy, in concert with the other parts, results in a net profit. A basic outline of the development of the wine list pricing policy might go something like this.

1. Establish how much gross profit the wine list needs to contribute to the business, so that with the bar and food operations, etc. all the costs are covered and (hopefully) there is a net profit. In established outlets this level of business can worked out with reference to past trading performance. In newly starting restaurants the forecasts must be made on anticipated demand in the business plan and later adjusted to account for actual performance.
2. Having established what sort of rate of return is required on the list, let's say 60%, then that standard mark-up can be applied across the board. To do this simply take the ex-VAT price from the merchant, add 60% and then add on the VAT at the end.

    Ex-VAT cost x mark-up percentage x VAT = Rough list price

    This leaves a rough idea of list prices, though neither rounded up or down to price points.
3. Using either past sales data or a forecast of likely sales patterns, establish what cash return such a list would provide. This is compared with the gross profit required from the wine list that was established in stage one. This must be done every time the list is adjusted to ensure that it is paying its way and contributing to the restaurant's total gross profit.
4. Adjust the list to account for the various market considerations. For example, if the standard 60% mark-up makes the Chablis £2 more expensive than all the other restaurants in the local area, the price should be adjusted down to account for the market. Furthermore, if another wine were £2 cheaper, then there is a case for making up the difference, leaving the wine still cheaper than elsewhere but contributing a greater margin. All the time recalculate whether the profit margins required from the wine list will be achieved, at least in principle. When doing this bear in

mind the concepts of elasticity of demand in that adjusting the prices of the big sellers and cheap wines will have an effect on demand that may actually reduce the cash contribution of that wine.

Price points

Everyone is aware of the policy of reducing products to the nearest 99 or 95 pence in an effort to make the product look cheaper. On a wine list this often looks tacky and commercial although the principle of using price points is important to create an effective list. First, the prices that have simply been marked up by a set percentage will be to the nearest penny; rounding up to the nearest 10 or 25 pence will create a neater looking list. Then consider whether to take the prices that are near a whole pound to just below that pound. Finally look at the structure of the prices on the list. Bearing in mind the old phrase of 'something to suit every pocket', try to adjust prices by rounding up or down to create an evenly priced list. If there are many wines at around £7 and £10 but few in between, try to adjust those nearest in price to fill this gap. Needless to say, in doing this it is vital to bear in mind the market considerations, elasticity of demand and the effects on the eventual gross profit contribution of the wine list to the restaurant.

The effects of a pricing policy

Only recently has wine been seen as something other than an adjunct to the main purpose of a restaurant – food. Good wine lists have been ignored in favour of good menus and restaurants have been marketed primarily on the basis of what food they serve and at what cost. Unfortunately this attitude invariably neglects wine when it could actually serve as a central tool in a restaurant's marketing. At the heart of this use of wine as a marketing tool is its price.

Consumer attitudes to wine prices.

Consumer affairs programmes and articles frequently refer to the high prices of wine in restaurants. This attitude appears to arise because customers compare the price for wine in a restaurant with the price at a wine merchant, particularly as they become more familiar with wine names and quality levels. This viewpoint is confirmed by the BBC Radio 4 'Food Programme' (19 May 1995) on the treatment of wines in restaurants. This constantly referred to restaurateurs as 'greedy' and implementing 'swingeing mark-ups'. Interestingly, both the wine writer Andrew Jefford and the show's presenter David Cooper, in conversation with restaurateur Neville Abraham, compared the prices in restaurants with those in high street wine merchants. Andrew Jefford, apparently going through a wine list in an unnamed (possibly fictional) restaurant, chooses:

> 'Koonunga Hill Shiraz/Cabernet, now that should be reliable, and there isn't usually much vintage variation with Australian wine. Yes, let's try that. What? £19.95, you can get that for under six quid in Oddbins.'

Derek Cooper remarks on the price of a Redcliff's Colombard Chardonnay, available at the time for £13.50 at Abraham's Café Fish and for £4.49 at the merchant Bibendum.

To market a wine list successfully, a restaurateur must either divorce the customer from the idea that the restaurant's prices can be compared with a wine merchant's or show how favourably the list prices compare.

Marketing wine using the price list.

Awareness of what consumers object to on wine lists makes the task of marketing considerably easier. For example, if the list carries wine brands that are not available at the large chain wine merchants then direct comparison of prices, like for like, becomes much more difficult. The drawback of this method is that customers are then faced with a list of unfamiliar producers' names. A second approach is to make clear how the wine prices are set and why. Increasingly, restaurateurs that formerly kept mark-up a closely guarded secret will now point out the wines that offer particularly good value (in the hope that the customer will buy two) or even explain certain parts of their policy.

The most common example of this is the flat rate mark-up over a certain level. The way it works is to mark up wines by a percentage amount up to a certain level. For instance, wines could return a gross profit of 60% up to say £10. Beyond this all wines are priced by adding £10 to the cost and adding VAT to the whole. This means that the prices of some of the very best wines in the restaurant are slightly or no higher than those in the high street merchant. This policy can then be used to encourage customers to buy better (and more expensive) wines on the basis that as they spend more, a smaller proportion of the price is profit. For the restaurateur the benefit is that customers will actually buy a better bottle of wine and contribute more to the profit than they would have done, even if the profit is smaller as a percentage of the cost of the bottle.

Philanthropic restaurateurs

Although it is hard to imagine, the general public's perception of high restaurant wine prices can be worked in favour of the shrewd restaurateur. By using an 'equitable' mark-up system and, more importantly, by publicizing it, an image can be created where the restaurant is seen to give very good value while at the same time actually earning more profit than its rivals. In consumer wine magazines and even the trade press there are often articles on good value wine lists that cast the owner as an altruistic soul intent on giving customers good wine, although not without a certain amount of self-sacrifice. This is extremely good public relations as it casts the owner as a wine lover, an image with which the public is far more comfortable than the money-grabbing business person.

SUMMARY

Wine control is a problematic area. Demand can be hard to estimate with stock difficult to control and then tricky to price to make a profit and still keep customers happy. This last area has become more sensitive as customers are increasingly knowledgeable about comparative wine prices in shops and restaurants. Within this environment the successful restaurateurs must control all wines from the moment they come into the restaurant to the moment they are sold. They can discover which wines perform strongly and put their effort behind them while perhaps removing those that are a drain on resources. Then with imaginative pricing the restaurateurs are able to use their wine pricing policy as a form of marketing.

QUESTIONS AND EXERCISES

1. What are the advantages and disadvantages of, in turn, cost plus pricing and market oriented pricing?
2. Describe the purpose of an Ullage Book.
3. Describe the ways in which wine might 'go off' through poor handling in a restaurant.
4. A restaurant goes through an average of 62 bottles of house white wine a week. It orders its wine about every two weeks and it takes up to one week for that order to arrive. The owner insists that there should be at least one week's stock of all wines in the restaurant at all times. At what level of stock should this restaurant order more house white?
5. Describe in general terms the passage of wine once it arrives at a restaurant, including what measures are taken during the passage to keep control of it.

FURTHER READING

Most textbooks on food and beverage management will contain chapters on practical beverage control, but two or three are worthy of note. *The Beverage Book* by Andrew Durkan and John Cousins (1995) covers a number of aspects of beverage control as well as basic introductions to some of the wine-producing regions of the world. *Food and Beverage Management* by Bernard Davis and Sally Stone is a well-established textbook on the subject, first published in 1985 and revised several times since.

Wines in the restaurant

PART 3

Developing a wine list 6

> *Key concepts*
>
> The main concepts covered in this chapter are:
> - writing the wine list;
> - practical considerations;
> - the wine list and the consumer;
> - marketing research.

INTRODUCTION

A failing of many textbooks on wine is that they discuss few of the issues about wine lists which really matter to restaurant managers. The first problem is that many books contain long sets of rules about the 'order of service' of wines. These rules were drawn up to help Edwardian diners enjoy sumptuous banquets. Few restaurant customers now ever drink more than one style of wine at a meal. Certainly the majority of the dining public never has the opportunity to enjoy dinners where nine or ten different wines are served, each with a separate course.

Second, many books are long on advice about very specific food and wine matches and mismatches, and rather short on discussing the general principles of developing a wine list. The job of the sommelier is to ensure that customers do not deaden the nuances of a delicate dish by choosing an acidic or harsh wine. The major concern for a manager in drawing up the list is to see that there is sufficient choice within it to find a wine that is a good match for the dish. Though it may sound mercenary, for the manager gastronomy is important insofar as it is profitable. Gastronomic considerations must work with the financial constraints of the business, its purchasing policy and, finally, what wines the manager (or sommelier) enjoy at merchants' tastings.

WRITING THE WINE LIST

The standard restaurant wine list format remains the most common way to list wines for the consumer. Long and comprehensive wine lists are divided by country, colour and price. In shorter lists, the separate sections for each country are omitted and red and white wines are shown in escalating price order.

The fact that this format is so common contributes to the dull uniformity of many wine lists. While much of this chapter and the next is devoted to breaking wine lists free from this uniformity, understanding of the format does give some basic conventions which, while less relevant today, are still expected by the consumer. This is the style of list with which consumers are most familiar. If a restaurant develops a list layout that is radically different, it can face the charge that the list is 'confusing' or 'complicated', even though it may well be far more logical.

General conventions are that red wines come before white and in most restaurants very sweet pudding wines are confined to a separate section at the back. This saves customers the embarrassment of ordering them by mistake to go with a main course.

Countries and regions are listed to reflect their importance to the wine trade and oenologists. France is invariably followed by Germany, Italy and Spain. Other countries follow according to either their importance to the list or the whim of the list writer. Few lists now leave out Australia and New Zealand and although the USA has lost its pre-eminent status as the top New World producer it frequently appears. For other countries a decision must be made about each as it appears. If the list contains a few wines from several different countries in a region, say Eastern Europe or South America, they are frequently listed together.

Conversely, with regard to the top four European countries – France, Germany, Italy and Spain – the number of wines may require subdivision into regions. In France the accepted sequence is Bordeaux, Burgundy, Rhône, Loire and Alsace. Then, depending on the number, either individual regions are listed (Gascony, Provence, Languedoc et Roussillon), or the whole simply headed 'French Country Wines'. Similar hierarchies for German, Italian and Spanish wines are less well defined, though certain regions do stand out in terms of quality and price. Often a region's status on the list will depend on the prestige of the wines within each category.

Wine list entries

The extent and detail of a wine list is very much dependent on the wines that are included and the style of restaurant. Unfussy restaurants that strive to give an uncomplicated 'meal experience' with good straightforward wines need only include the very minimum information on their list. In smarter restaurants that serve much finer wine, customers expect to find a list that gives much more detail.

In general it is always a safe rule to try and keep the list as simple as possible without missing out any important information. Below are details of items sometimes included in wine list entries. They are not all essential (although wine name and price obviously are) but should be used according to the style of restaurant and wine list. These include:

- bin numbers;
- names;
- classification;
- vintage;
- descriptions.

Bin numbers

These usually appear first, on the lefthand edge of the list. They correspond to the position or bin card of the wine in the cellar. They serve two useful purposes. First, they make it easier for customers to order wines, particularly if they have a complicated name. Second, they make finding the wine easier for staff, particularly if unused to dealing with wine. Simply dealing with a bin number saves them the trouble of having to write down wine names, not to mention avoiding mistakes when there are several vintages of the same wine, or wines with similar names. Also when billing customers for their meals, whoever makes up the bills simply has to read a number rather than a foreign name in someone else's writing.

Names

At the very least a wine list should show a wine's name and price. This is the name as it appears on the label of the bottle. In Europe the wine's name is usually the *appellation* (e.g. Chablis, Rioja, Barolo) followed by the producer (e.g. Louis Michel et fils, Marqués de Murrieta, Fontanafredda). In the New World wines tend not to have an *appellation* but are known by a combination of grape variety (e.g. Shiraz, Cabernet Sauvignon), brand name (e.g. Koonunga Hill, Pelorus) and producer name (e.g. Penfolds, Cloudy Bay). Wine names are notoriously fickle and there is a multitude of exceptions. To ensure that the list gives each wine its proper name, pass the wine list to the merchant for checking or look up the wines in the merchant's list or a wine reference book.

Classification

Classifications change from region to region and are sometimes incorporated into the name of the wine, but they should always be included in the wine description. On the whole only Old World producers have classification systems. The most common are those that guarantee the authenticity of the wine. France was the first to introduce a wine authenticity system with its AOC (Appellation D'Origine Contrôlée) classification, which is the basis of all European systems.

- AOC (Appellation d'Origine Contrôlée) – France
- VDQS (Vin délimité de qualité supérieure) – France (lesser quality)

- DOC (Denominazione di Origine Controllata) – Italy
- DOCG (Denominazione di Origine Controllata e Garantita) – Italy (guaranteed quality)
- DO (Denominación de Origen) – Spain
- QbA (Qualitätswein bestimmter Anbaugebiete) – Germany
- QmP (Qualitätswein mit Prädikat) – Germany (better quality levels)

When listing German QmP wines it is important to give the quality level or 'prädikat' for which the wine qualifies. In order of sweetness (and quality) these are:

- Kabinett
- Spätlese
- Auslese
- Beerenauslese
- Trockenbeerenauslese
- Eiswein

Other classification systems include Grand Cru and Premier Cru status which will be listed on the label. Some regions also have their own classification systems. The most famous of these is the 1855 classification of Bordeaux estates which divided them into five classed 'growths', with others classed as Exceptional, Bourgeois and Artisan Growths.

Under current EEC rules Premier and Deuxième Cru classes remain on labels with other Cru classes simply labelled 'Cru Classe'. Of the lesser estates, Cru Exceptionelle and Cru Bourgeois are still found, though Cru Artisan is rarely seen.

Vintage

Vintage is the difference between wines from different years and wherever possible this should be included. All but the most ordinary house wines (and non-vintage champagne) are from a specific vintage. Given the vagaries of nature, in some wines (not least those from the great regions of northern Europe) vintage variation can be great. Even in regions such as Australia, where technology and a consistent climate minimize vintage variation, it is important to include vintages so that customers can be confident they are not approaching a wine that is too young or too old.

Restaurateurs face several difficulties by including vintages. Throughout the year merchants will run out of current vintages and move on to new ones. It may be that the new vintage is inferior to the last – a problem which can only be resolved by tasting. The second problem is that the list becomes incorrect. Unfortunately vintages do not all change at once. The list may require alteration several times during the year to update vintage information. Although not ideal, one way to reduce the number of changes is to list both the current vintage and the next one together (e.g. 1988/89) so that concerned customers can ask which vintage is current. This policy should be restricted to relatively ordinary wines and not extended to the very finest quality wines on the list.

Descriptions

The description remains the most contentious part of wine list writing. Descriptions of the taste and style of wine are inevitably subjective and as such risk running contrary to customers' impression of the wine or raising their expectations only to find the wine ordinary by comparison. Apart from descriptions of taste, some lists use information such as press comments or the scores of wine writers like Robert Parker. These have the benefit of deriving from independent sources, but some customers may find the writer in question irritating or disagreeable.

Some of the best descriptions are those of irrefutable fact. For instance, few can object to details of where the wine is grown, interesting facts about its history or connections with famous people. Alternatively, some find information on good food and wine matches very useful.

Perhaps the guiding factors in whether or not to include wine descriptions are the knowledge and numbers of staff. In a restaurant with a specialist sommelier to attend to each customer's wine choice, descriptions are superfluous. In a much smaller, more informal outlet where staff are not wine experts and have little time to devote to wine sales, useful information on the list can help the customers to make good choices on their own. In such a case a little research and some help from the wine merchant are advisable.

Separate wine lists or menu and wine list combined?

Throughout this chapter (and in fact this book) reference has been made to wine lists as though they are always a separate entity, but this is not always the case. Nor are wine lists only attached to menus in less prestigious restaurants: the wine list and menu are combined at Raymond Blanc's new Brasserie.

There is a number of practical advantages to having a unified menu/wine list. The number of 'lists' in use in a restaurant is reduced. Staff are spared the embarassment of not knowing to whom to give the wine list if the host is not obvious. Customers only need to consult one list rather than two, which is an advantage when trying to make decisions about the various combinations of food and wine to be enjoyed.

A unified list can be a disadvantage if there is a large number of wines on offer. A very large wine list incorporated into a menu makes it bulky – undoubtedly drawing comments that it is more like *War and Peace* than a menu. There is also the disadvantage that every change to the wine list involves amendment of every menu. Although reprinting the menu (or even the offending pages) may not be required each time, this can be one more responsibility for the busy restaurateur. In time heavily amended wine lists look messy and are more prone to mistakes. Fewer wine lists mean that more time can be spent on updating them and keeping them in good condition.

For restaurants with a limited wine selection, a combined menu and wine list is a sensible option and adds to the informal atmosphere. Where the wine list is much larger it is far more practical to keep the full list to a separate document. However, to promote certain wines or to make choice easier for those who do not want to wade through the full wine list, a partial list printed with the menu can be a great success.

Matching the wine list and the menu

One danger faced by many restaurateurs is that their merchant will give them a 'formula' wine list. This will contain all the same styles of wine, if not the same actual wines, as every other restaurant in the area. When presented with such a list customers are not tempted to try anything new or to 'trade up' to a better or more interesting wine. They just go for 'old-favourites', which are invariably well-known wines that rarely offer good value for money. The customer inevitably goes away disappointed. To overcome this problem it is important to start by matching the list to the menu, perhaps introducing some sort of theme or, in other words, putting some thought into the list.

Classic matches or versatile old favourites

One way of introducing some variety is simply to add on to the usual list of well-known wines a few that are slightly out of the ordinary. This is particularly useful if the wines are chosen to go especially well with a certain dish on the menu. Good examples of this are sweet wines from Australia and the USA that provide perfect accompaniments to chocolate, orange and Christmas puddings – all difficult foods to match with wine. Customers feel comfortable faced with a familiar choice of wines but can be tempted into an additional spend on something out of the ordinary.

Alternatively consider finding a really perfect match for a house speciality. For example, Alsatian Gewürztraminer is often heralded as a 'trade secret', partly because it is a little more expensive than many table wines and partly because of its very individual taste. Yet this wine is a very good match with Chinese food and spicier dishes. If there is a suitably spicy 'house speciality' then it is worth selling this (slightly more expensive) wine as a perfect match.

Specialist restaurants

For restaurants that serve a particular national cuisine try to create a wine list which continues the theme. For instance, Italian wines are invariably the best matches for Italian food. It is certainly worth trying to find specialist merchants to supply restaurants serving national dishes.

Less obvious specialist lists are those required by oriental restaurants. The spices and delicate flavours of the food can make many wines taste flat, acidic or harsh. As mentioned above, Gewürztraminer makes an ideal match. Other Muscat varieties can also work well and it is worth exploring them to find more interesting matches. The list may end up more concise but it will work.

Vegetarian restaurants are often just left with very straightforward wine lists that not only lack character but are not even vegetarian. Eggwhite and isinglass, taken from fish, are both routinely used in the production of wine to precipitate solids left after fermentation. Furthermore while many vegetarian restaurants choose only organic produce for the kitchen they can end up with wines that have been sprayed with a variety of chemicals. Finding organically grown and produced wines can be difficult as few producers release such details about the production of their wines. To overcome this, the main body of the list can be made up of wines that are good but with an unknown provenance. Then mark out particularly those few wines known to have been produced organically.

A variable list or a long-lasting list

Few things are more irritating to customers than ordering a meal, finding a wine that appears to be a perfect match, and then discovering that the restaurant no longer stocks it. There are two ways of overcoming this problem. The first is to gain assurances from the supplying merchant that the wine will remain in stock, and at a reasonable price, until the next review of the wine list. Some merchants have a reputation for selling out of particular wines while they are still on restaurant lists. It is always a good idea to pick up some 'local gossip' to find out if anyone is particularly notorious.

The second solution is to have a policy of deliberately changing the list, or part of it, periodically to keep it fresh. This is made easier by word processing and graphics packages on home computers which allow restaurateurs to turn out professional looking wine lists or supplements whenever they wish and at very little cost. This also means that the restaurant can take advantage of small lots of wine picked up at auction or not normally offered by wine merchants because supply is so irregular.

Concise or comprehensive lists

In many quarters there is an unchallenged view that a very long, complicated list with a multitude of expensive wines and several vintages of the same wine is necessarily a good thing, and that with the extended choice goes customer satisfaction. This is not necessarily true. The London chef Nico Ladenis writes in *My Gastronomy*:

> I have never been able to understand why people go into rapture and ecstasy over the wine list of a restaurant which is pages long. In the last 20 years, the surge of great food and great restaurants has been accompanied by the phenomenon of the short menu. Short menus make it possible for a chef to cook well and to concentrate on a handful of spectacular dishes. Why should this not apply to wine as well? Why not a short, well-thought-out wine list?... In our Battersea days we overheard someone saying we had a bad wine list. When the subject was raised later, this charming know-all admitted that what he really meant was that it was a short wine list, not that all the wines on it were bad.
>
> (Ladenis, 1997: 46)

At the very least, in crude financial terms, the capital needed to buy and remain tied up in storing large amounts of wine means that the long list needs to be more profitable than a shorter one. Such a list requires close management to prevent stock levels getting out of hand and to maintain some sort of financial control to calculate performance levels. Ultimately though, a large number of very similar, moderately priced wines only confuses the majority of customers, while many expensive wines simply extend the choice for very wealthy customers at the expense of those drinking cheaper wine.

PRACTICAL CONSIDERATIONS

When restaurateurs have combined what is suitable for the restaurant and menu, using the criteria above, with what is available from the chosen merchants (as discussed in Chapters 3 and 4), they will begin to have an idea of what their wine list is going to look like. The next factor in shaping the wine list is to decide what is practical for the restaurant to carry.

This is largely a question of the length of the wine list. To develop Nico Ladenis' comment, there comes a stage when the benefits of a long list are outweighed by the problems of its management. The ideal wine list provides a selection of wines to suit most tastes which will combine well with the food on the menu. Adding superfluous wines that are only occasionally sold merely satisfies those customers who enjoy looking through extravagant lists. For the restaurateur all they do is confuse those customers who are not knowledgeable about wine while making the rest of the list less efficient and harder to manage.

Storage

For many restaurants storage will be a major limiting factor to what is carried on the wine list. To establish how many different wines the cellar can cope with is a matter of combining the total capacity of the cellar with the numbers of each wine that are required. To establish these numbers, use the formulae for calculating stock levels given in Chapter 5. To work out the stock levels these formulae rely on the demand for each individual wine, demand that will be diluted to some extent by increasing the choice of different wines on the list. However, it would be foolhardy to assume that by creating a more extensive wine list, storage space for the new wines can be found by reducing the stock held of all the others. A more extensive wine list invariably means reduced stock turnover and with it more stock lying around. It is always the case that extending the wine list involves more storage space.

Financial constraints

In the same way that a long wine list needs more storage space, it also needs greater financing. Unless the increase in wines on the list is matched by an equivalent increase in bottles sold (and as people see wine as an accessory to a meal, not central to it, this is unlikely), the rate of return on the money invested in wine will decrease. The extra bottles that lie in the cellar do not earn anything and are of questionable value in promoting the image of the restaurant, a defence sometimes used by those who want a long list.

The wine merchant's terms

Along with financial and storage considerations, the wine merchant's terms create some absolute limits on what range of wines the restaurant is capable of carrying. Limited space for wine storage is not a problem for a restaurant that has wine delivered several times a week. If deliveries are only once a fortnight, a limited list of high sale wines whose turnover can be predicted accurately is the only option. Equally, credit terms that allow much of the wine to be sold before it is paid for increase the available capital for a more extensive list. On the other hand, paying by cash-on-delivery limits the funds available and forces the wine list to perform more efficiently.

The abilities of staff

The wine knowledge of staff can be crucial to a restaurant's success in selling wine, particularly fine wine. It is a simple fact of human nature that people who buy very expensive, fine wine enjoy discussing it with the sommelier and being fussed over a little as it is decanted, tasted and poured. If the staff treat it as though it were house wine, not through any malice but simply lack of knowledge, customers become dissatisfied and feel they have not had value for money. Equally, good sales technique is vital to sell more costly wines. As the price goes up, the customer becomes more 'involved' in the purchase. Convincing them to buy the wine requires good product knowledge and confident assurances that they will enjoy it. The product knowledge should be sufficient to ensure that customers are not sold a bottle of wine that clearly they would not enjoy or would be a poor match for their food choice. Confident assurances from staff that they will enjoy the wine, perhaps drawing on personal experience, will put customers in the mood to enjoy it. If they feel nervous that their choice could be an expensive mistake because the waiter or waitress did not appear confident in recommending the wine then they will be less inclined to enjoy it.

THE WINE LIST AND THE CONSUMER

It is not unusual for wine lists to be chosen by only two people – the restaurateur and the wine merchant. Yet the lists are intended to satisfy the different tastes of thousands of customers. Many who draw up wine lists make no attempt to recreate market conditions or give consideration to what the market wants.

Wine lists are drawn up using a mix of intuition and personal preference for a variety of reasons. Wine is still 'shrouded with mystique' for many. As a consequence it is felt that only those few invested with a sensitive palate, wine knowledge and tasting skills can choose wine. Second, wine is often selected on the basis of building up a list of passable wines at low cost, rather than trying to find anything truly worthwhile. Low cost high margin wines that are very popular with customers are often dismissed as being 'tacky' or 'cheap'. Finally, wine is still seen by many in the hospitality industry as a consumer interest, at best a hobby sometimes indulged 'professionally' by gourmet restaurateurs, but nonetheless a hobby. Such an attitude leads many to believe that wine is not a fit area in which to apply rigorous business disciplines like marketing research. Rather it reinforces the idea of the wine buff as expert, capable of making choices for the masses, bringing the situation full circle. All the wine for a restaurant is chosen by a committee of two – the restaurateur and the merchant.

MARKETING RESEARCH

Marketing research is a complex subject in its own right, taking up entire textbooks. For the purposes of this chapter, marketing research is limited to its applications in wine list management. It is often said in marketing circles that there is never enough money to research all the information required to make management decisions; resources must be allocated where they can be of most use. Thus in cases where the information yielded by the research could have an impact on a major revenue earner for the restaurant, marketing research can be money well spent. In other cases, where the decisions made can only have a limited impact, these must be made on the basis of intuition.

Unfortunately, the problem for restaurants is that their wine lists are often created solely on the basis of intuition and with no hard facts to back them up. Yet wine is not a minor revenue earner and restaurateurs routinely see all their net profits coming from these lists. To ensure that the list proves popular with customers (and thus profitable) requires some targeted research on what the consumer wants.

All marketing research uses a basic five-stage process:

- decide what information is needed;
- find the sources of relevant information;
- collect the information;
- analyse and interpret the information;
- report and use the research findings.

Deciding what information is needed

This is simply the problem that needs solving. In a new restaurant it is 'what wines should we have on our list?' In an established restaurant it may be 'what can be done to increase sales of wines in the middle of the price range?' or 'which wines should be dropped to give space to new discoveries?' The most important aspect is that there is a definite and achievable aim to the research. All the way through the research process, return to this initial goal. If any of the information yielded or avenues being pursued are not directly relevant then put them to one side and return to the core question set at the beginning of the exercise.

To help the definition of what sort of research is being conducted consider to which of the categories below it belongs. These will define the research processes and information sources that are needed later on.

When is the research carried out?

- **Routine research.** This is the tracking of sales information and other data to monitor the success and profitability of the wine list. Regular analysis using the Grid Group Analysis system to monitor wine performance (Chapter 5) would come under this category. Equally, using the information from good beverage control to yield information would be applicable.

    Because this is ongoing research, the collection procedure must be part of the day-to-day or weekly business of the restaurant. Unless collation happens regularly there can soon be a backlog of data and data that are incorrect. For example, in the collection of data for Grid Group Analysis, failure to include the figures from a particularly busy bank holiday weekend could produce seriously misleading information involving future planning.
- **Occasional research.** Occasional research answers specific problems on a one-off basis. The most obvious example is that of the restaurateur who is just starting up in business and needs to decide what sort of wine (what price, what quality, how much choice) to include on the wine list. Alternatively, established businesses may conduct occasional research prior to a wholesale change of their list, a repositioning to attract a new market or before special events like wine promotions or Christmas and bank holidays.

What is the research into?

There is research that answers questions about the environment in which the wine list has to work. It asks about the local area, who lives there and what sort of competition the wine list is up against. It considers the customers and what makes them want to spend their money, what wines they already buy and whether they could be persuaded to buy something else. This research asks questions about the wider business and economic environment; trends in consumption, changing habits, new products and fashions.

Alternatively there is research into the marketing mix, those tools or methods that can be used by the restaurateur to manipulate demand for the various parts of the wine list. Commonly called the 'four Ps' these are:

- Product;
- Price;
- Promotion;
- Place.

Product research may be considered in two ways. Primarily it involves research into the popularity of both existing and proposed new wines. For the restaurant though the popularity of the wine list is not just based on the individual wines but the list as a whole, and as such may be considered the 'product'.

Pricing research considers the prices in comparison with those in competing restaurants, on both a like-for-like level as well as the general wine pricing strategy. It can also consider the elasticity of demand of wines and the effects of changing pricing policy.

Promotional research encompasses the design of the wine list (itself an important promotional tool) through to research into the feasibility and success of specific promotional events. Wine tastings and talks are increasingly used by restaurateurs to generate new customers and increase restaurant use during quiet times of the year. To make sure that these events are successful, marketing research into the best method of promotion and after-the-event analysis check that the money has been well spent.

In this context place or distribution research concentrates on stock levels held in the cellar and the effect of different suppliers' delivery systems. In larger outlets with several sales areas it includes the physical distribution of stock about the building(s). In hotels and units with several different sales areas analysis of distribution can also encompass the make-up of different wine lists. For instance, if a bar has a smaller potted version of the main restaurant wine list, research could look into the effects of having one all-purpose list or two totally separate lists.

Finding the sources of relevant information

Commonly divided into two categories, primary and secondary, the sources of information used in any project will depend entirely on the research to be carried out.

Primary sources are those that collect new information. Examples of this are questionnaires and interview groups. Collecting this sort of information is often costly and time consuming and, in the context of wine lists, of limited value.

The one exception to this rule is tasting panels. These provide vital information on individual wines. At the start of this section I mentioned the problem of a restaurateur and merchant choosing wines for a list in glorious isolation. The problem of this approach is not they might have flawed palates but simply that the two of them will always find it hard to make decisions about what people will like. By increasing the numbers who taste a wine, the broader base of opinion will give a better impression of how the wine is likely to sell. What is more, if the panel uses restaurant staff, this approach involves those most likely to have to sell the wine day by day.

In choosing those involved in a tasting panel try to gather as many people together as possible. Previous tasting experience is almost to be discouraged as the opinions needed are not what the wine tastes of so much as whether the panel enjoy it or not. Give them the wines blind and possibly use some sort of very basic scorecard. This might only note whether the wine is good or bad and how much the respondent feels it is worth, but nonetheless it does keep a record for later reference. Initially, taste in silence so each person makes an independent verdict on the wine, but do allow discussion later. Ensure that the verdicts given in the silent tasting are not adjusted to take account of the general sway of opinion during the discussion stage. It is only natural for people to try and come up with the 'right answer', but this is of little use to the restaurateur looking for unbiased opinion.

With the exception of tasting panels, easier and cheaper information for many restaurants and hotels to obtain, and often of far more use, is that from secondary sources. This uses information that has already been collected, some of which will be specific to the individual restaurant such as sales records and patterns. As mentioned above, collection has to be a continuous process and very much part of the daily routine of the restaurant. By and large this is quantitative information, in other words it deals with the amounts and value of wine sold. Since choice of wine is so much a matter of taste, qualitative information is also of great importance. Wine tastes change and in order to follow their trends it is vital that restaurant managers are well informed of recent developments.

Information on what rivals are selling can be invaluable. Try to get hold of their wine lists and keep track of any special promotions. Comparing prices against those of rivals can yield useful information about why usually popular wines are not selling very well. If one restaurant is heavily out of line on one particularly popular product it can give an impression that the whole list is overpriced. A collection of merchants' lists, even if they are not suppliers, is also very useful. These will show what sort of prices and terms are on offer elsewhere and, in conjunction with restaurateurs' own lists, can yield information about rivals' mark-ups.

As wine is a product that is very heavily guided by fashions and fads, restaurateurs, especially those keen to give a fashionable meal experience, will need information on the latest products and trends in the marketplace. Some statistical information is available in guides such as *The Drink Pocket Book* (annual), as well as special reports in trade magazines, principally *Harper's Wine and Spirit Gazette* and *Wine and Spirit International*. These magazines also contain features and trade news, although they are aimed at the retail wine and spirit business rather than hoteliers and restaurateurs. For a limited amount of wine information aimed directly at the on-licensed trade, *Caterer and Hotelkeeper* has a wine column and occasional features. However, many restaurateurs still use the consumer-based wine press, despite the fact that its bias towards the consumer gives little information about the saleability of the wines featured.

Collecting the information

Fortunately collection of secondary information is far easier than primary since it merely involves finding the source and lifting out the relevant pieces. Primary information collection is a specialized task that is often carried out by specialist marketing research firms.

As indicated above, the only source of primary information regularly used by restaurants is tasting panels. The samples involved are not so large as to make full-scale statistical analysis worthwhile or even feasible, but to prevent them becoming biased it is important to make sure that the initial tasting is done individually and without discussion. Any written record of the panel's opinions should be taken away before discussion begins.

Analysing and interpreting the information

Again primary sources of information can be measured using complex statistical methodology that is quite beyond the scope of this book and of little use to all but the very largest hotel groups. In analysis of the sort of data that the above methods are likely to yield it is worth remembering the following points:

- Any analysis of sales data must account for exceptional periods of sales such as Christmas. Quite apart from involving very high sales of wine, these periods are also likely to involve very uncharacteristic sales patterns in terms of the types of wine sold (e.g. much champagne is sold over Christmas).
- Ensure that the information yielded answers to the initial question. As already stated, the first thing to do is to set a clear aim for the research. Return to this aim and ask if it has been achieved.

Reporting and using the research findings

A cynic might say that much marketing research is conducted in order that managers might have something to blame when their decisions go wrong. If sales figures fail to pick up they can always say, 'but we conducted proper marketing research so it isn't our fault'. As mentioned at the start of this section, managers can only expect marketing research to act as a tool to help them in their decision-making, especially in something as fickle as the wine market. But managers must be brave enough to use the research when it points in a particular direction.

If a bizarre sounding wine from a new producing country receives top marks from all the staff during a blind tasting then it is foolhardy to override that opinion just because it appears to be a bold move to put it on the list.

SUMMARY

In the past the very finest hotels and restaurants would have had lists containing wines from around the world to suit every palate and every dish on the menu. Today this sort of wine list is impractical (too many countries produce wine to make it feasible), very costly and not a valuable selling point.

Modern wine lists must be built around a variety of factors. They must match the menu, giving both classic matches and interesting combinations as well as very versatile wines that go with a wide range of dishes. The number of wines on the list will then be limited by storage space, available money, abilities of the staff and the wine merchant. Once all these wines have been selected they must be described adequately and attractively on the wine list.

A concise wine list must therefore target its consumers more accurately. Many restaurateurs do this already, though frequently it is in a rather piecemeal fashion. Wines are bought on a 'hunch' or because they seem fashionable rather than because the restaurateur knows that they will sell well. To overcome this approach restaurateurs must find out exactly what it is that their customers like. A variety of tools can be employed including tasting panels, sales data and publicly available sources of information. Correctly interpreted, this sort of market analysis can be invaluable in helping to guide what goes on a wine list and what it is worth forgetting.

QUESTIONS AND EXERCISES

1. What information should be included on a wine list and why? What information could be left off to make the list less 'wordy'?
2. Describe the different ways that wine may be named on its label.
3. From your own experience, list some great food and drink matches. These need not be well known classics or even involve wine (curry and lager) but be specific and list as many as you can.
4. In a group, list half a dozen different foods or dishes; try to ensure that there are 'modern' fashionable foods as well as older dishes. Without consulting each other, list what wine would go with each dish. Once everyone has written their wine matches come together as a group and collate the results. See if there is any consensus across the group for certain dishes. Is it fairly indistinct (white/red) or more specific (Chardonnay/ Champagne/ Claret)? Do the wines listed tend to be famous old names, wines the individuals have drunk recently or wines learnt about recently in class?
5. Another group exercise is to ask one person to write a wine list entry *for the same wine* in four different styles: as brief as possible; in a wordy, highly descriptive style; listing factual information about the region; and finally in an amusing style – perhaps finding a pun in the name (not funny admittedly but frequently found in wine lists). Then ask each member of the rest of the group to list three terms that describe each style and rate it between one and ten. Again analyse the findings to see which is the most popular (and least) and what terms were applied to that description. A structured group discussion can help clarify why they liked (disliked) the description.

FURTHER READING

As food and wine matching is such a personal thing, much of the literature tends to contain personal testimonies rather than acting as authoratitive guides. For information on 'old-fashioned' rules of food and wine matching, I would recommend *Practical Professional Gastronomy* (Cracknell and Nobis, 1987). For a more personal view, a book such as *My Gastronomy* by Nico Ladenis (1987) is by turns amusing and informative.

7 Merchandising wine

> *Key concepts*
> The main concepts covered in this chapter are:
> - they know everything but what it tastes like;
> - innovative ways of selling wine;
> - creating a merchandising strategy;
> - alternatives to straightforward wine list sales.

INTRODUCTION

The problem at the heart of all wine sales is that until the bottle is opened, the customer has no idea what it is going to taste like. Wine purchases have to be made on trust — either trust in what the wine list says about a wine, trust in the customer's own knowledge of wine, or trust in what the sommelier recommends. This chapter is about methods of engendering that trust and creating more adventurous and higher spending customers.

THEY KNOW EVERYTHING BUT WHAT IT TASTES LIKE

In this chapter we concentrate on three ways of encouraging wine sales. The first is simply to make the choice easier, by highlighting or promoting one particular wine or a limited selection.

The second is to work a way around the problem of the 'unknown in the bottle'. It is much easier to convince someone that they will enjoy a new wine if they can try it beforehand. The difficulty of doing this with wine lies in its perishability. After only a few hours open and in contact with the air a wine will begin to go off. By using a range of new products, wines can be left opened under blankets of inert gas or with much of the air removed, thus preserving them for days and even weeks without deterioration.

Finally, the chapter deals with endorsements. Many customers lack the confidence (or wine knowledge) to make a decision about a choice of wine. They are much happier if their decision is backed up by the endorsement of someone 'in the know'. Comments by wine celebrities, gleaned from the wine magazines are useful for list descriptions and point of sale material described later in this chapter. Alternatively, recommendations by staff, particularly in relation to food and wine combinations can lift customers out of the rut of always ordering the same wine.

Conservatism and customers

Most restaurant customers will have at best a fairly limited knowledge of wine. Many restaurateurs with extensive lists become disappointed when only half a dozen wines ever seem to sell while the rest lie in the cellar tying up cash. The reason for this is that although there are vast numbers of wines available, most people try one, find they enjoy it and can remember its name, and they stick to it. They are intimidated by the mystique of wine, afraid of choosing something they may not enjoy, and of making fools of themselves.

Such customer conservatism has both benefits and drawbacks for the restaurateur. The benefits are that with little effort a wine list can be drawn up that is bound to satisfy (though not excite) almost everyone. The sales from the list are predictable and any wholesale merchant could provide a continuous supply of the wines on the list.

The drawbacks are that everyone in the chain of supply knows that these wines are popular and capitalizes on the fact. By the time these wines arrive at the restaurant they offer very poor value. To try and offer a list of every customer's old favourites at competitive prices means that the margins on the wines have to be cut right back. Pandering to such customer conservatism guarantees sales, but at little return.

Adventurous customers and profitability

The alternative to an 'old favourites', low margin wine list is to develop a streak of wine adventure in customers. This has benefits both in the behaviour of customers and the performance of the wines. The choice of a wine that is 'a bit different', particularly with friends, makes it more of a treat. By playing on the 'treat value' of the wine purchase, they can be persuaded to spend more.

For example, if customers normally drink German white wine, they are experts in German white wine. They know how much it 'should' cost, and their opinion of restaurant's list is based on the price of that wine. The availability of the wine means they will have bought it to drink at home; they will know its off-trade price which gives them an indication of the wine's mark-up. If for a change (influenced by one of the merchandising methods below) they choose a similar style of wine from elsewhere in the world, an Italian 'abboccato' for instance, they have no prior conceptions about it. Not being familiar with its price they may spend more, and if it is a success will return to drink it again, the 'discovery' of a new wine standing out far more than the mere enjoyment of an 'old favourite'.

For the restaurant there are also benefits. Unfamiliar wines have to provide better value to enjoy sales. Very high quality wines are frequently sold cheaply because nobody trusts them. But with good merchandising these wines can be sold on to customers as cheaper, better alternatives to their favourites. They will still turn in a healthy profit on the basis that the wine merchant has to sell them more cheaply because restaurants are cautious of taking them on.

INNOVATIVE WAYS OF SELLING WINE

Wine was always meant to be fun, to be enjoyed and help create a good atmosphere. Yet this image of wine is hard to reconcile with the dull, yellowing lists of names that feature between so many old plastic wine list covers. There is no mystery about why so many wine consumers only ever drink one or two styles of wine. Nobody has ever tried to convince them to drink anything else. If young customers increasingly drink beers and spirits during meals, it is because these drinks have a more accessible, exciting image.

For many the only reason to drink wine during meals, even after the so-called 'wine revolution', is because it is still the done thing. But this is not a market led approach and restaurants will find that, as older more traditional customers are replaced by younger ones, wine sales, for so long the great money earner of the restaurant business, will decline.

To halt this decline those selling wine must listen to their customers and must tell them what they have. It is no longer enough just to leave a wine list on the table and expect the profits to come rolling in.

The sorry state of wine merchandising

The main tool in any wine sales armoury is the wine list. Aside from the actual content of the list (Chapter 6), the look of the list must be right. Shabby, dirty or yellowing lists do not inspire confidence in the reader; rather they give a sense that if the list looks like this, then the wines are probably a pretty sorry bunch as well.

Yet the list is often the only tool that restaurants have for promoting their range of wines. Apart from simply being tatty these lists also fail to meet the needs of the customers, and not just by having the wrong sort of wines. For instance, in popular informal restaurants there are long complicated wine lists with no descriptions of the wines – leaving the average customer with little idea of where to start, let alone what to choose.

Conversely, restaurateurs that have the potential to attract wine loving customers, and to make much of promoting their wines, let themselves down by providing an inadequate wine list. Inadequate here does not mean a list that is too short (if anything concise and well chosen lists are better), but one filled with cheap wines, tacky descriptions and poor quality pictures.

Finally, even restaurants that do have well laid out wine lists that are suitable for their target audience and kept neat, clean and fresh looking, fail to gain sales because the customers are not fully aware of what the restaurants have to offer. Wine lists suffer from the problem of being simply lists of wine. They consist of names laid out in some sort of order for customers to choose from. Unless the customer is fascinated by wine, this choice requires concentration and effort.

If customers are distracted, in the middle of conversations or greeting people as they arrive, the temptation is simply to order bar drinks or the 'house wine'. But if they are prompted by well thought out material, they should be induced to order the wines being promoted. The advantages of this approach mean that they will drink a wine that the restaurateur favours and hopefully remember the good wine they had, rather than some ordinary house unmemorable 'plonk'. Second, the promoted wine is chosen by the customer for its convenience, not for its price or name. Therefore, without going over the top, the restaurateur can choose something with a good cash margin as well as quality, making it more profitable than simple house wine.

Methods of wine merchandising

Merchandising is 'any form of behaviour-triggering stimulus or pattern of stimuli, other than personal selling, which takes place at retail or other point of sale' (Buttle, 1986: 3).

Within this definition there are some important aspects to note. The first is that it does not include personal selling. The skills of staff in wine selling are discussed in the next two chapters and have their own vital role to play. Unfortunately, the role of personal selling by staff sometimes overshadows efforts to implement merchandising opportunities. This can lead to just the sort of problem described above. While personal selling is vital for customers who want to discuss the wine or where the staff have the time to devote to it, in the real world customers are often tied up in their own conversations and just want to order whatever is easiest.

This is where merchandising becomes important. By using a 'behaviour-triggering stimulus or stimuli', the restaurateur saves time and interruption of customers in the middle of conversation. They buy good wine without even knowing they have done so. Furthermore they buy profitable wine, unaware that there is any pushy sales effort.

Setting merchandising objectives

Before implementing specific wine merchandising tools, restaurant managers must decide why they are implementing a merchandising strategy and what they want to get out of it. This means that merchandising objectives must be set. With wine sales these objectives can be both specific or general. Specific objectives are the most obvious as they centre around specific products: for example, 'to increase sales of the Rioja by 10% during July'. Here the objective is to increase the sales of this specific wine, by a measurable amount, within a given time period.

General objectives relate to wine sales as a whole, perhaps: 'to increase average wine spend per table by £1 during the next two months'. Again though, the objectives are clearly defined even though the objective is general in its outlook.

Note that in each of these examples the objective is quantifiable and over a stated period of time. At the end of that period the restaurateur can evaluate the success or failure of the exercise by using the relevant sales data and comparing them with the initial objective.

The principles of good merchandising

The principles of creating any merchandising tool have been described by Buttle (1986: 390) using the mnemonic ASDA:

- accessibility;
- sensory domination;
- appeal.

Any merchandising tool has to make the promoted product accessible to the customer. Returning to the example of the customer who is greeting friends and wants to order some drinks, by making one particular wine more accessible than the others by the use of a promotional tool, the customer will choose that wine because it is more convenient, more accessible.

Sensory domination in wine sales is usually limited to sight. At the risk of sounding over-simplistic, this is the sense that sees tent cards, special offers and highlighted parts of the wine list. Of the other senses, wines neither appeal to the customer nor vary too much by touch. Hearing is unsuitable because restaurants are places where people expect to make their own conversation and not be interrupted by announcements about wines on offer.

Smell and taste are the only other senses that are very useful, but are sometimes hard to apply in practice. A superb way of convincing customers to buy a wine is to allow them to taste a little first, but this involves opening a bottle which will in time deteriorate. Methods of preserving bottles to overcome this problem are discussed later.

Third, any merchandising must appeal to the customers. Giving them a taste of wine will lead to a desire for more, particularly if the amount is tantalizingly 'just a taste'. Any written or visually stimulating material must appeal to the customer on a more psychological basis. The design of any visual merchandising tools must take into account the restaurateur's target market, desires and aspirations. In much the same way as designing the wine list will take into account the likely wine knowledge of customers, promotional material will similarly have to appeal to what they know and enjoy.

Finally, merchandising should be an ongoing part of the routine of the restaurant, but must not become 'part of the furniture'. The routine should assess what times of the year any merchandising technique is likely to have the greatest impact and restrict it to that time of the year. Constant promotions, point of sale material and sales drives soon lose their impact. When customers expect there to be some special offer, the restaurant will merely maintain market share or sales targets by promoting different wines. Merchandising must be kept fresh, monitored while in operation, and then withdrawn at the end of the stated period and its success evaluated.

Tent cards and other point of sale material

The easiest and, for those with the facilities, perhaps the cheapest way of merchandising wine is with specially printed point of sale (POS) material. Left out of this category are all the more permanent items like blackboards which are dealt with later. This category includes the most common device, tent cards, as well as specially printed posters, wine list inserts and other short-term, disposable cards.

With a personal computer and a basic graphics package it is an easy task to run up simple merchandising cards. Tent cards are usually around four to six inches long, two to four inches high, and promote a specific wine or two. There is no need to go over the top on detail; the name and vintage of the wine, its price, a simple description and perhaps a good food partnership are all that is needed.

Alternatively some restaurants use tent cards to give the customer more detail about a specific wine. If the day-to-day wine list is a simple one, listing names, vintages and prices but nothing more, tent cards give an opportunity to describe a wine or producer in detail. This is particularly useful if the restaurant is promoting a more informal image, or around Christmas when there are people coming in who rarely eat out during the rest of the year. Large parties like to choose these wines as they are selected for their broad appeal and the choice is made easier for them.

Tent cards can be kept clean either by lamination or being kept in special plastic holders. Laminated cards certainly look nicer, while permanent holders give the impression that there is always a wine promotion.

Within the wine list, merchandising material again either highlights a wine as a special offer/recommended choice, or else provides a detailed description of one of the wines in the list. If the restaurant carries a number of different wines from the same producer, a description of the producer and their techniques somewhere on the list can provide added interest and help sell the wines.

The psychology of wine sales comes into play, as customers learn more about the product and feel more confident about ordering it. A brief narrative about the wine informs customers without the need to ask the sommelier. It also gives them something to talk about when the wine arrives. Some restaurants build up relationships with producers (or their importing agents), who then pass on information to help write these pieces or their own promotional material to incorporate into the list. Such 'evidence' of a special relationship between the restaurant and a specific supplier acts as a strong incentive to buy. Again, commonsense caveats apply in that the restaurant can only have a 'special relationship' with one producer and must be genuinely convinced that the product is top quality and good value.

The choice of wines for this sort of merchandising obviously depends on the objectives set during the planning stage. Certain objectives are particularly suited to this style of merchandising.

Bulk sales of wines that provide better margins than house wine are especially suited to tent cards. Say the objective were to increase wine spend per head over Christmas, then tent cards would prompt orders for that wine rather than house red or white. Tent cards will also help to develop wine sales in this way during the year but, again, use them judiciously or the promotional effect will be lost. One way to emphasize the temporary nature of the promotion is to have a seasonal choice. In the autumn, when menus might include game and 'heartier' dishes, use tent cards to point out what good matches are the richer, heavier red wines (Château neuf-du-Pape, Australian Shiraz, Barolo). These wines are often slow sellers as many modern lighter dishes are overpowered by them, but matched with suitable foods they create more memorable meals for the customer because they are different.

Finally, tent cards are very useful for gaining additional sales of 'pudding' wines which are often offered by the glass (discussed below) or in half bottles. Few customers order pudding wines unless prompted in some way. Stuck at the back of the list these wines are easy to miss anyway. The problem is exacerbated as starter, main course and wine are ordered at the same time.

DESSERT WINES BY THE GLASS

'For decades fine sweet wines have been the least appreciated and most undervalued of the world's great wines' (Brook, 1987: 7). In the first line of his classic book *Liquid Gold*, Stephen Brook identifies one of the great truths of the wine world. Not only is it unfortunate for consumers that they do not enjoy the many superb sweet wines that are produced, but also for restaurateurs it is a great missed opportunity. A glass of sweet wine can turn an ordinary pudding into something sublime and greatly enhance the consumers' experience of your restaurant and possibly bring them back for more.

Undoubtedly there have been three great disincentives to putting sweet wines on a wine list. First, sweet wine has been associated with cheap, poorly made German table wine. This had had the effect not only of bringing down the consumer image of German sweet wines, but also of all other sweet wines. Enjoying dry wine is always considered estimable, but sweet wine is rather more problematic as consumers seek to distance themselves from the poor image of much commercial sweet wine. Second, people want to drink less alcohol generally, and are discouraged at the thought of having an extra bottle at the end of a meal (even in a large party). Finally, in an attempt to overcome these hurdles many considered serving these wines by the glass — but this ran the risk of the wines going off before they were finished.

Fortunately by-the-glass technology has advanced in recent years and a number of systems have evolved to preserve wines for several days after opening. It is now up to restaurateurs to put on promotions that make the best use of these advances. They should capitalize on the fact that sweet wines make outstanding matches with puddings and have a certain rarity or 'treat' value.

> **CHRISTMAS**
>
> Christmas is such an important time for all restaurants that it is vital not to miss a single opportunity for additional sales. At this time of year many parties need little or no encouragement to buy a great deal of wine, but do not be lulled into thinking that there is no need to work hard on wine sales. A 5% increase in value here would dwarf the effect of a sales push at any other time of year. Switching sales from house wines to better margin lines is one way of increasing profit. Selling wines that are ignored for the rest of the year is another. Champagne and other sparkling wines are not only popular as celebration drinks but are more price elastic. Pudding wines, which are usually ignored for the rest of the year, can provide very good matches for the sweet foods (mince pies, Christmas pudding). One style in particular, Australian Liqueur Muscats, provides heavenly matches. As well as making every effort to sell these to prebooked groups, POS material should highlight them and again emphasize their 'treat value'.

Nobody is thinking of desserts at this stage and certainly not of wines to go with them. When the desserts are ordered, few restaurants offer the list again as this may appear pushy. If a small card is placed on the table, particularly for a wine that is a brilliant match with one of the puddings, the waiter or waitress can allude to it without giving an impression of the hard sell.

Wine of the month

Wines of the month are a useful tool outside the peak times of the year for generating sales. They can be advertised using any of the POS methods: tent cards, list inserts, or blackboards. In using the term wine of the month, make sure that it is only promoted for that period. The strategy risks discredit when customers in June realize that the wine of the month has not changed since February. Also, choose a wine with some fundamental reason for being 'wine of the month'. Beefy, alcoholic red wines are useless in the summer and no amount of being wine of the month is going to increase their sales. Instead choose a rosé or light aromatic white that would go particularly well with seasonal menus.

Special offers

The practice of providing free wine to sell meals is increasingly used by restaurateurs to promote flagging sales during weak periods. These special offers can reap rewards if they are properly managed but must be treated with great caution.

First, define exactly the terms of the offer and make them absolutely clear in any promotional material. Ambiguous or unclear language could lead to customers being misled. This not only leaves them frustrated but may also be in breach of the law.

Second, work out the costs of the operation very clearly and search for any loopholes in the terms of the offer. The tight margins on food can easily lead to the cost of the wine taking up all of the cash margin and the restaurant may even end up with a loss.

Third, consider what the public image of the offer may be. For the restaurateur it can be a simple case of lifting bookings in a quiet part of the year. For the general public the offer may signal that the restaurant is in trouble financially and is struggling. Furthermore, nobody expects free wine offers to involve quality wine. One effect of the offer could be that customers associate the wine list with the free wine, rather than with the actual quality of the wines on it.

Bin ends

Bin ends are a tool that is used rather unimaginatively and often proves more of a bind than a bonus. Bin ends are defined as those wines that have come to the end of their supply or are being delisted in favour of something else. To get rid of bin ends and make space for the new lines, restaurants either return them to the merchant or sell them cheaply to customers and/or staff. Instead, they could create sales, for example, by selling them either at cost (plus VAT) or a large discount to big parties or regular customers. This sort of bin end offer can be sold to regular customers as a 'loyalty bonus' for their continued custom by sending a mailshot to tell them about it. Those wines that are cheap enough could be used as part of a short-term 'free wine with meals' deal. Either way, the wines should be used to generate business, not just sold off as quickly as possible.

One ever present problem for those who sell wine is the wines that go 'off'. When wines reach the end of their shelf life, use the bin end term to sell them quickly at a discount. Some people are tempted to sell the wine using the 'wine of the month' label. Preserve this term for wines that are genuinely of good quality. If a faulty or 'past it' bottle is sold as a bin end it can be explained away as a problem of choosing a bargain and simply replaced. If the wine of the month becomes associated with whatever the restaurant wants to get rid of, then the term is devalued.

Special purchases

Special purchases are not so much a merchandising tool for individual wines as a way of merchandising the wine list as a whole. The category of 'special purchase' includes any wines which are not normally part of the list but bought outside the usual ordering routine. The best example is wines bought at auction, perhaps only in two or three case lots. Alternatively, as small boutique producers in Australia and New Zealand find demand for their wines soaring, their agents and wholesalers release these wines on a strict allocation basis.

Rather than turning down the chance to list these wines because of their short supply, make a feature of it. Use a list insert to point out how these wines are limited and how lucky the restaurant is to get hold of them. The insert enables the restaurateur to list the wines without having to change the wine list every time one of them runs out. It should also point out that the customer is lucky to have a chance to drink these wines and that the restaurant works hard to bring them these gems.

Before listing special purchase wines, and particularly if a great feature is going to be made of their rarity value, make sure that there is a demand for them and that they are genuinely rare. A restaurant ends up looking foolish if the wine list proclaims it has sourced a rare wine and the customers have seen it elsewhere – particularly if the other restaurants have not made a feature of the wine's rarity value. Also it is not much of a special purchase, short-term wine if it is still on the list months later.

In restaurants with a strong clientele of regular customers, special purchase wines can be used like bin end offers as a 'loyalty bonus'. With the increasing fashionability of some wines from boutique producers, customers find a certain social cachet in having drunk them when their friends have not. For example, let us say a restaurant has six cases of the most famous New World boutique wine, New Zealand's Cloudy Bay Sauvignon Blanc. Simply putting the wine on the list may result in many happy customers over the next month or so who enjoy it with their meals. However, such a strategy fails to maximize the marketing potential of this sought-after wine. A better plan would be to make the most of the supply and try to maximize the sales of meals around this wine. An alternative strategy would be to invite all the restaurant's regular customers to buy tickets for a tutored tasting of the wine led by a local friendly wine merchant, or possibly a Master of Wine or wine 'celebrity'. Obviously, the more famous the 'tutor', the more the ticket price would be. At the tasting the restaurateur should include other comparable wines from New Zealand and around the world, as well as serving some canapés. As part of the offer, give all those present the chance to enjoy any of the wines featured (including the 'stars' of the show) at a meal in the restaurant over the next few weeks. Thus, instead of simply placing the wine on the list, generating no new business and possibly risking the ill-will of regular customers ('What, you had Cloudy Bay but you've sold out, and there is none left for regular customers like us?'), careful use of wine merchandising will have generated two fee-paying events, additional to regular business, and plenty of client goodwill.

CREATING A MERCHANDISING STRATEGY

The merchandising strategy of a reastaurant brings together all the elements laid out above with one guiding principle: keep it fresh. Merchandising does not work if it becomes routine. Regular customers start to expect it and staff forget it and fail to put in the personal sales effort to make it work.

To ensure that merchandising remains fresh, each component must be conceived and directed with this as the basis. Equally each of these merchandising plans must act as a coherent whole, so that throughout the year staff and customers are constantly drawn to sell and buy the wines that are merchandised. Typically a wine merchandising year might go something like this:

January: A traditionally quiet time of year after the New Year celebrations, so promotions should be generated in April to attract custom generally rather than lifting sales of specific wines. It is at this time that 'free wine with meals' promotions are most often used. Overstocks of wine bought for Christmas can also be sold, perhaps as part of a special promotion for regular customers.

May: To ring the changes as summer approaches specialist tastings are useful events to bring people into the restaurant.

June: The tastings can be arranged in conjunction with events such as a new wine list to promote those wines that are particularly noteworthy. Tent cards can highlight particularly good food and wine matches as the increase in seasonal produce changes the look of the restaurant's menus.

July/August: In high summer capitalize on people's thirst and the continental image of al fresco eating by featuring wine by the glass, half bottles, and large amounts of chilled whites and easy drinking rosés. Depending on the location and type of trade, promoting wine in these formats can increase lunchtime business. By selling the most 'quaffable' wines in unfussy formats such as the jug or carafe, it is possible to sell a great deal of high margin wine in the evenings.

September: During the autumn themed menus and wine matches are an ideal way to extend the drinking repertoire of customers. If asked, many people will admit to drinking only a very limited number of styles, partly because these are most readily available in high street wine merchants. As a way of weaning customers off the ubiquitous Cabernet Sauvignon and Chardonnay onto flavoursome but less common grape varieties such as the white Marsanne or reds like Nebbiolo, link them with menus that feature the heartier autumn flavours of game and root vegetables.

December: The most important thing to bear in mind when developing a plan for Christmas promotions is that the best way of generating repeat business is to give a memorable experience. Alongside the more elementary side of Christmas merchandising such as tent cards, prompting customers into purchasing a more profitable and better quality wine, try to give them something different. If marketing a Christmas lunch as a whole package, include in the deal a glass of sweet wine (Australian Liqueur Muscats are perfect) to go with the Christmas pudding. Although many people say that they do not like sweet wine, this is often because they have not tried it or have tried it out of context. The introduction of sweet wine as part of a Christmas package requires no 'hard sell' on the part of staff and no conscious decision on the part of customers to be adventurous.

Throughout the year the promotions provide extra interest and keep customers and, more importantly, staff happy. Before each promotion the staff can taste the wines that are being merchandised and help in the effort with personal selling. Telling the staff a little about the wine means that if a customer asks about a tent card they can follow up that initial interest with their own knowledge and close the sale.

ALTERNATIVES TO STRAIGHTFORWARD WINE LIST SALES

Much of the purpose of merchandising is to remove the customer's reasons for not buying the product. In most of the examples above the methods of merchandising are all instances where customers are made aware of a wine without having to open and concentrate on the wine list – the accessibility component of the ASDA mnemonic (Buttle, 1986: 390).

However, with wine there is an additional component – merchandising must overcome the problem that wine is served in a bottle. The bottle must be opened for any kind of product sampling and once opened the wine begins to deteriorate. Allowing customers to try wine before they buy is fine in principle but can result in a large amount of wasted wine, eating up all the profits generated from the wine sold. Yet the attempt to sell anything different from the cheapest or most well-known wines on a list is often an uphill struggle in the face of customer conservatism unless they can try it.

Offering wine in different formats

The term 'different formats' means the offering of wine in amounts and containers other than standard bottles (by-the-glass sales are dealt with in more detail below). Methods of serving several glasses of wine include:

- different bottle sizes;
- carafes and jugs;
- wine on tap;
- larger bottle sizes;
- wine by the glass.

Different bottle sizes

Different bottle sizes are perhaps most commonly associated with Champagne, which is often sold in sizes equivalent to as many as 20 bottles or 15 litres (a Nebuchadnezzar) or as little as a quarter bottle (20 centilitres). Different sizes are rarely seen in the UK except to contain sweet wines. Although much of the blame for this omission can be laid on the producers (the margin on smaller sizes is reduced), some of the fault also lies with those selling wine who fail to promote them adequately and create a market.

By far the most common alternative size of bottle is the half bottle (37.5 centilitres). Giving roughly three good glasses as opposed to the full bottle's six, they are often used for lunchtime service or where only a small amount of wine is wanted for a starter while a full bottle is ordered to go with the main course. A merchant with a good range can supply a large proportion of wines in both full and half bottle size, as well as a number of wines in just the half bottle – sold perhaps as ideal for lunch. The disadvantage of the half bottle size is that it is not enough – it is a good quantity for one person alone during an evening, but not quite enough for two people at lunch.

If half bottles are not quite enough for lunch, half litres are slightly closer to the mark. The problem for the UK restaurateur is that, given the traditional British dislike of drinking at lunchtime (or drinking beer if they do), this size and others commonly found on the continent are a rare find in most wine merchants.

Carafes and jugs

When selling large volumes of cheap and cheerful wine it is often worthwhile to provide it in open carafes or jugs. This means that the wine can be bought in any quantity desired, as long as there is a means of preserving it, although the volume will lead to economies of scale through bulk purchases. The benefits of this style of selling are that it is informal and very effective if trying to promote an unstuffy image. As the wine is bought not for its name, it need not be of outstanding quality, though be cautious of amazing deals in case the wine is in some way faulty. Only buy wine that is genuinely pleasant to drink and fault free and look particularly for chemical odours or signs that it might soon deteriorate through oxidation.

Wine on tap

Although wine on tap often becomes 'wine by the glass', it is included here as the next section really concerns quality bottled wine by the glass. At the risk of sounding dogmatic, it is fair to say that any restaurant keen to promote itself as a seller of quality wine will shun wine on tap. Most commonly found in pubs, the quality of the wine is usually dubious, even as a mixer for which it is often used. If the wine were good enough to be sold by the bottle then it would be. But this wine is chosen not for its quality but for its profit margin by large suppliers and brewers. Given the far superior quality of so many good value bottled wines, there seems little justification for choosing poor quality wine on tap.

Larger bottle sizes

Although the main thrust of this discussion is concerned with smaller bottles to encourage boldness in customers' wine buying, it is worth remembering that larger sizes can also work. These are often bought when groups of customers are celebrating – note the wide variety of shapes for Champagne, the ultimate celebration drink. Stocking a magnum of other wines can also be successful. Large parties enjoy the image of opulence and extravagance that magnums lend to the occasion. Their size gives them the image of a good value purchase, which very often they are. Good staff training to ensure that possible 'magnum customers' know they are available will produce healthy sales of these profitable wines.

Wine by the glass

This is by far the most versatile selling tool in the wine sales armoury. It overcomes two problems that prevent people from buying wine in a restaurant. The first is that they need not finish a whole bottle. Increasingly, drinking at lunchtime in any quantity is frowned upon so unless there is a large number of people a whole bottle may be problematic. Second, and more importantly, many customers hold back from ordering wine because they are afraid of what it will taste like. Ordering wine that tastes unpleasant is seen as a social faux pas, so many customers order the same wine over and over again because they know what it is likely to taste like. If wine can be bought by the glass there is less of a stigma, and if it is not to their taste they will not feel that they have wasted too much money.

Unfortunately many restaurateurs only provide two or three wines by the glass (perhaps a red, and a medium and a dry white), restricting the rest to bottle sales. The quality of these limited wines is frequently mediocre, leaving customers who want a better quality of wine the problem of having to buy a bottle. Two strategies are useful for developing the sales value of wine by the glass sales:

- provision of 'tasting' glasses;
- allowing customers to try a variety of wines.

Provision of 'tasting' glasses

The availability of a wide range of wines representing a number of styles by the glass, offers customers the opportunity to try a wine before they buy a bottle. If this facility is combined with staff training, it becomes more than simply 'try before you buy' and develops into a useful sales technique. By offering customers the chance to try more expensive, better quality wines than the ones they might usually choose they may be encouraged to 'trade up'. Alternatively, if the customers have ordered their food and find it hard to agree on the wine, an offer of the opportunity to try something interesting (and profitable) may persuade them to make this their choice rather than the compromise of a house red or white. As mentioned before, when customers are given the occasion really to enjoy wine in a restaurant, they will remember it more clearly, return and recommend the restaurant to their friends.

Allowing customers to try a variety of wines

Undoubtedly one of the reasons why wine consumption is moving further towards 'standard' popular wines, such as the ubiquitous Cabernet Sauvignon and Chardonnay produced in an international style, is because people rarely take more than one, possibly two, styles of wine at meals. A large table may have a white wine (Chardonnay) with the lighter flavoured starters, followed by a red (Cabernet Sauvignon) with the main courses. These wines accompany a very wide range of foods and, although perhaps not providing the perfect match, they make for a pleasant enough combination. By offering a wide range of wines by the glass, the restaurateurs can give customers the opportunity to enjoy a really superb combination without having to buy a whole bottle. The best and most common example is the provision of dessert wines by the glass. Too often these are flabby and overpriced Muscat de Beaumes de Venise or a poor quality, sugary white Bordeaux. Instead, restaurateurs should offer something really interesting and try to combine it with a menu choice. For instance, if the local merchant has a small number of bottles of a particularly good sweet wine, take it on and merchandise it alongside a particular food combination. Although some customers may be slightly disappointed that they cannot order this wine and food combination the next time they come, try to have a similarly good combination in its stead. Alternatively, offer customers particular wines by the glass as they order their starters. Again, by generating interest in the meal and giving customers the chance to enjoy truly fabulous combinations at minimal cost, they will leave happy and eagerly return.

Preservation methods

The main reason why restaurateurs are unwilling to hold a large number of wines available by the glass is the worry that they will go off and have to be thrown away. Before considering any of the preservation methods currently available it is worth understanding just what process is taking place when wine does go 'off'.

The main culprit is oxygen. Oxygen is both the friend and foe of wine producers and wine lovers. It can help to produce some of the finest wines in the world and allow them to live for centuries. Yet it can also destroy many of the wines commercially available in a matter of days once they are exposed to the air.

Traditional wine-producing regions such as France, Spain and Italy have often used oxygen as an aid to gaining complexity in wine during its production. They allow the grapes and must contact with the air and then mature the wines, in some cases for several years, in oak barrels. This results in wines that lose some of their freshness but are robust and complex with long shelf lives. Some Madeira, the fortified wine from the island of the same name off the coast of Africa, can live for as long as two hundred years and remain drinkable, partly because of its high acids which act as a preservative, but also because they are deliberately oxidized, or maderized, during production. While only a minute proportion of the wines of Madeira are capable of this length of life, they do illustrate the point that the wine maker can produce wines that remain pleasant and drinkable for several days after opening.

Unfortunately for the restaurateur, these wines which have been exposed to oxygen are not to the taste of most modern wine drinkers. Part of the phenomenal success of the wine producers of Australia and California has been to produce wines which exclude the action of oxygen as much as possible. Right through from when the grapes are picked (in the middle of the night when they are not taking in oxygen) to the closed vat fermentation of the must, everything is done to preserve the flavours of the grapes. This method produces wines that are fresh, fruity and easy to drink and has proven enormously successful to a whole new generation of wine drinkers. But these wines are susceptible to the action of oxygen once the bottles are opened and certainly are meant for drinking within the first year or so of their life. If they are left open a variety of reactions takes place that initially turn them brown (maderization), leaving the wine with none of its initial freshness and eventually making it vinegary.

There are several methods available to slow down this degradation of the wine so that a bottle can be used for up to several weeks after opening, with the wine tasting the same or only minimally different. These include:

- vacuuming;
- nitrogen blankets;
- wine boxes.

Vacuuming

This is the most common method and the one most often seen in the home. The idea is simple, given that air is the problem, simply remove as much as possible from the bottle. The methods range from small hand-held instruments that are sold for use in the home to larger, commercially available pumps which include integral refrigeration units. As well as cooling wine to the desired temperature for the customer, this chilling also has the advantage of slowing down the oxidation process.

Many restaurateurs spoken to during the research for this book found this the most reliable and efficient system, as well as the most cost effective, so long as the rubber stoppers supplied were regularly washed to remove sugars from the wine that built up over time and prevent a proper seal from forming in the bottle neck.

Nitrogen blankets

These systems use an inert gas (that is one without smell or taste which does not react with the wine) to cover the wine or fill the empty part of the bottle to prevent oxygen getting at it. All the systems use nitrogen. Again these come in both domestic and commercial versions. Smaller domestic units might simply be a small canister of the gas (the size of a can of fly spray) with a nozzle designed to fit wine bottles. Once the gas has been squirted in, the bottle is recorked until needed again. Larger commercial units require a much larger canister and a series of tubes so that the appliance can serve a number of bottles.

The main problem levelled against these devices, not least the commercial units, is that the large number of tubes and their joints provides ample opportunity for the gas to escape, gas that is entirely odourless and colourless.

In one example, a unit that served six bottles had 30 joints per bottle, 180 in total. If one leaked, nothing would be discovered until the pressure gauge on the canister fell to indicate that it was empty and another was needed. Then all 180 joints on the system had to be checked to see which was faulty.

Other methods

Wine boxes are generally available for the domestic wine lover, but can be useful in a commercial setting. The wine is contained in a bag which shrinks as the wine is tapped off. Wine stored in boxes would be a superb solution were it not for the fact that the wine is so often of poor to mediocre quality. The availability of such average wines rather contradicts the subject of this chapter, which is to convince customers to try something more interesting.

Chalk boards

This chapter earlier covered a number of different printed methods of merchandising wine, but deliberately left out the more temporary method of writing on a blackboard. This is a favourite of many restaurants for a variety of reasons:

- The wines featured on the board can be changed quickly and often.
- Unlike printed material, wines listed on boards can have their prices or vintages changed without rewriting the whole list.
- Blackboards are favoured because they fit in very well with the whole image of wine sales. They are rustic, changeable and slightly old fashioned. For this reason they are more suitable than more modern neon boards sometimes seen in fashionable wine bars.

Expert and celebrity endorsements

Much of this chapter has dealt with quantity of wine as a merchandising tool. As well as giving customers the opportunity to buy wine in smaller quantities without having to finish a whole bottle, wine served by the glass allows them to overcome any fears about whether they will like it before buying more.

The customer is looking for an assurance that the wine is not going to be foul and they are not going to look a fool. This explains the popularity of so many newspaper wine columns. Restaurant and retail wine customers feel far more confident about buying a bottle of wine if a trusted authority (even though most wine columnists are not exactly household names) has pronounced it a good buy.

Unfortunately, unless customers have the column with them they can rarely remember the name of the wine being recommended. If restaurateurs are to use these press comments successfully they must integrate them into the wine list. Two ways to do this are either to add the quotation as part of or instead of the description of a wine, or else to make a feature of 'recent press comments' elsewhere on the list. The list of comments can be kept current by the periodical addition of new ones and removal of those that are out of date. A short sublist of wines with press comments is a useful way of recommending wines other than the house wines. Staff can allude to it for customers who want something out of the ordinary but not too expensive.

A certain degree of research is necessary to find enough press coverage to make this exercise worthwhile (having only one wine commented upon can look derisory. Most press comment about wine comes in the specialist magazines (*Wine* and *Decanter*) and the weekend newspapers. Ask staff and friends to cut out the relevant sections. As a wine merchant I used to record any television programmes that featured wine (BBC's 'Food and Drink'), not only to make sure that we did not miss out when wines we stocked were featured, but also to be able to quote accurately the comments of the presenters. The phrase 'as featured on television' can work wonders for a wine's sales.

One word of warning for those using this form of merchandising: ensure that you would recommend the wine as vigorously as the presenters or writers. One criticism levelled at those who recommend wine in the media is that they have a vested interest in 'talking up' as many wines as possible. Many producers send wines direct to the writers or invite them on expenses paid trips to the country. Writers do themselves a disservice if they have a reputation for being unduly harsh on wines because this can limit the number of future invitations. While careful selection of a wine supplier and proper wine list development will ensure a good list, just make sure that the comments bear some relation to the wine you have.

Staff endorsements

Staff endorsements can often be as effective as celebrity endorsements, but they do run the risk of sounding precious and/or arrogant. Avoid rather starchy comments like 'Your host this evening recommends', or a sublist under a flowery title saying 'The Chef's Choice'. Staff recommendations are best restricted to informal lists where there is already a certain amount of comment and should be restricted to people the customers might know like the sommelier and the proprietor.

SUMMARY

The merchandising of wine has two objectives. The first is to sell more wine, and to sell better (more expensive) wine. The second is to make the consumer's experience more memorable. This may sound rather trite, as though on one side restaurateurs are emptying the customers' pockets while on the other they are telling themselves that the customers enjoy it. However, such an analysis does not do justice to the added enjoyment of the customers. Instead of buying a second-rate wine plucked from the many on a wine list, they are 'sold' an interesting match for the food they have chosen and a wine that they will remember after they have left the restaurant.

The methods of wine merchandising are diverse, presenting a wide range of opportunities for restaurateurs to try. If one approach does not work or becomes stale over time there is always another that can be tried. Furthermore the variety of methods for merchandising wine range far beyond those covered in this chapter and could be event specific (such as a one-off sports/cultural event) or specific to the location of the unit. What is needed is a certain amount of imagination and a determination to 'sell' wine to customers, rather than simply letting them choose from an anodyne list.

QUESTIONS AND EXERCISES

1. Design a tent card to sell a hearty red wine of your choice in the autumn. You could relate any text on the card to menu items or simply seasonal factors. Make sure that it is striking and appealing to the eye, but gets the message across to the customer that they should buy this wine. In your design take account of the fact that the more complex and colourful your design, the more expensive it would be to produce.
2. Construct a Christmas wine sales plan. In it include a rough design for a tent card, an insert to the wine list and a brief that you will give to staff to help them convince customers to trade up to specially promoted wines. You must also select wines to go with a classic Christmas menu. You must decide what wines you are going to promote.
3. What objectives does wine merchandising seek to achieve?
4. Describe how you would try to merchandise:
   - a bin end;
   - a sweet pudding wine;
   - Champagne;
   - house white;
   - a wine recently featured on a television programme.
5. Describe the various benefits and disadvantages of 'wine by the glass'.

FURTHER READING

Francis Buttle's *Hotel and Food Service Marketing* (1986) contains a very useful chapter on merchandising in food service outlets (Chapter 20), and is based strongly on the marketing theory behind merchandising practice.

Wine service skills 8

> **Key concepts**
>
> The main concepts covered in this chapter are:
>
> - the process of wine service;
> - theatricality in wine service;
> - dealing with disasters;
> - training in wine service.

INTRODUCTION

This chapter explains why certain things are done the way they are, not just to help to understand the process of wine service but also to show how wine service can be less stuffy and more informal. Waiters and waitresses often worry about whether they are 'doing it right' or that they will be shown up because of a lack of knowledge.

THE PROCESS OF WINE SERVICE

When establishing the operating methods of a restaurant it is vital that a standard procedure for wine service is incorporated into them. In the rush of service it is all too easy to forget that a table has not been looked after. It is far easier to remember to return to a table to take the food order because this has to be delivered to the kitchen. In the case of a wine order, the responsibility for which may not be clearly defined, it is simple to forget under the pressure of food orders. This is not how the customer sees it. They will very often want their wine to drink almost straight away (even though it is usually ordered after the food), and certainly before their food arrives.

To prevent any confusion, when planning restaurant operating procedures and allocating responsibilities, the following items should be taken into consideration.

- Who has responsibility for taking wine orders and wine service?
- Does the waiter or waitress take the food order or a sommelier?
- When is that order taken?
- What happens when a customer wants to order wine at some other stage in the procedure, for instance, as soon as they come into the restaurant?
- At what stage during the meal should different wines be given to the customer?
- How are staff briefed on the merchandising of particular wines and the opportunities for personal selling?
- Which wines on the list make particularly good matches with the current menu?
- What is the procedure for out of stock and temporarily unavailable wines, and how are staff briefed on this?

Planning for every eventuality in this way may seem to be overzealous. But if it can be done the slick service that comes into play with difficult situations and customers, reflects well on the restaurant and will undoubtedly lead to repeat business.

Presenting the list

The wine list goes to the host of a party. It is both patronizing and infuriating for a woman who is taking men out for a meal to find that the wine list has been given to a man in her party. If in doubt, always ask the member of staff who took the table booking or greeted the party or else ask the party itself who is the host or would be choosing the wine. It is always wrong to assume the host will be a man.

It is at this stage of presenting the list that it is possible to start selling the wines. Identify those that are being specially merchandised or are on offer. If any wines do provide especially good matches with particular foods, point them out. Most importantly do not leave the list with customers for them to choose something mediocre or ordinary if there is the possibility of selling them a wine of better value. Do ensure that good communication skills are employed. The customers should not feel that they are being given the 'hard sell', or have their conversation broken up by over-attentive staff.

When the customer gives the order write it down on an order pad, with the top copy going to the cashier and the duplicate to the dispensing bar. In drawing up the operating procedure bear in mind the following points:

- What happens if a customer asks for a wine list before or after they are given the menus? This must be done promptly and efficiently; it is irritating for customers if staff look confused because 'that's not the way we normally do it'.
- If the list carries pudding wines, do ensure that customers are given the opportunity to notice and buy them. If not giving customers the whole list again, see that a separate card with pudding wines on it is presented when they are given the puddings.

Presenting the bottle

Presenting the bottle and tasting it are the two most misunderstood parts of wine service. The object is to show customers the bottle before it is opened so that they can confirm that it is the wine they ordered. Therefore do not open the wine before presenting it to the customer. The reason so many restaurants do this is because they lack the confidence to open a bottle in front of a customer, but this defeats the whole object of presenting it in the first place.

When presenting it, bear in mind that customers may well have forgotten exactly what it was they ordered, so to avoid an embarrassing silence fill in by describing the wine to them, perhaps dropping in some piece of information about the wine or its producer. When doing this try to look interested, particularly if waiting for the customer to get out reading glasses. It is not uncommon to see staff glancing nonchalantly round the room while they wait with bottle in hand. The customers are paying for you to make a fuss of them, so humour them.

As in so many service situations, try to read what the customer wants. Some people abhor the fuss and procedure of examining the bottle while others adore it. Customers usually give fairly strong hints about what they prefer, and they enjoy their meal so much more if you can pick up the hint.

Opening bottles

First remove the capsule, that is the metal foil or plastic cover over the neck and cork of the bottle. Opinions vary as to whether or not the foil should be removed above or below the collar, the raised ring of glass at the upper end of the bottle's neck, or even removed entirely. By far the most presentable and neatest way is to cut the capsule below the collar. This allows you to make sure that the whole area is clean and tends to lead to a better cut. Also ensure that:

- the foil is removed cleanly and the cut edge has no jagged edges which are both unsightly and dangerous;
- enough of the foil is removed so that it does not come into contact with the wine while it is being poured from the bottle.

Once the foil is removed put it in a pocket or receptacle until it can be thrown away. Next wipe the exposed top of the bottle with a cloth. If this is particularly dirty use a damp one. This is to remove any mould or lead salts (see below) that can taint the wine as it is poured out. It is important to do this before removing the cork. If it is done afterwards there is a tendency for any solid bits to fall into the wine.

Next remove the cork. Always use a corkscrew with a wide 'worm thread' rather than a 'gimlet screw'. Gimlet screws have a solid core and sharp edges which cut and split the cork, making it crumble and hard to remove. Worm thread corkscrews – common on the 'waiter's friend' style corkscrew – are much gentler on the cork and far better with fragile corks. When inserting the cork ensure that the thread goes down the middle of the cork. Squeaking noises are often the sound of the thread sliding down the glass. Although often unavoidable, stop screwing the thread in before it comes out of the other side of the cork. When the corkscrew emerges at the other side it can dislodge small pieces of cork into the wine that look unsightly in the glass which is poured for the host. This often elicits the mistaken question of whether the wine is 'corked' (see box).

When drawing the cork the trick is to try and draw it in a straight line. Most corks break when the corkscrew twists at an angle with the bottle and the half-removed cork cracks in two.

Once the cork is successfully removed, pour a little of the wine for the host to taste. If they accept it serve the wine to their guests. The reason for offering some wine to taste is that in the past, when wine quality was far more variable than it is today, the host could ensure that the bottle was not faulty. While the process of tasting still gives the customer the opportunity to reject a faulty bottle before it has been poured out, such cases are rarer. Today the custom is frequently shunned as fussy and unnecessary. If so, simply move straight on to pouring out the wine. Very occasionally customers will reject a perfectly decent bottle with the claim that there is something wrong with it when really they just do not like it. Good customer care usually dictates that the wine is replaced with something else.

> The head wine waiter at the Ritz in Piccadilly, Luigi, has described himself as a salesman. He sells what he wants and not what the customer wants. His example of this power is when a customer has ordered a wine but, on tasting, does not like it. Luigi replaces it with the same offending wine.
>
> (Finkelstein, 1989: 57)

> We very rarely get involved with customers when they complain about a wine. We simply provide a new bottle and send the offending one to our wine merchant. Invariably, the answer comes back that there is nothing wrong with the wine, there is something wrong with the customer! The whole point is that when a customer, in our experience, normally complains about the quality of a wine, he is not saying that the wine itself is at fault. All he is saying is that it is not to his taste, which is what he should have said in the first place and is a very different thing.
>
> (Ladenis, 1987: 45–6)

Opening champagne and sparkling wine

This requires caution and care. The pressure inside a bottle of sparkling wine is around 70 lb per square inch and can force the cork to fly out very quickly. Every year people are injured by carelessly opened sparkling wine bottles. In a restaurant where one could be held liable for such personal injury extra care must be taken. Essentially, little can go wrong so long as the cork is kept under control at all times and is always pointing into empty space.

You will need a glass and possibly a napkin. Hold the bottle at 45 degrees.

> **LEAD AND WINE**
>
> Lead does occur naturally in grapes, particularly those grown near roads where they take in lead as they respire from exhaust fumes. This lead is removed from wine (as with most heavy metals) during fermentation, but can be introduced to the wine at later stages; this has been the subject of some speculation in recent years. For restaurateurs the two relevant sources are decanters and the necks and foils of bottles. Cheap decanters, notably those from certain parts of Eastern Europe, can release lead from the glass into the wine, although evidence suggests that this is only significant if the wine is left for periods longer than usual or is drunk in vast quantities. A study of port 'left in a lead crystal decanter for 4 months' had a strength of lead concentration that '10 l of it would have to be consumed in a short time for a potentially toxic human intake of lead!' (Robinson, 1994: 558).
>
> More important for the restaurateur is the possibility of lead contamination from the capsule. This possibility seems to be minimal, but by removing the capsule from *below* the collar of the bottle and wiping away any lead salts that have built up on the neck of the bottle it is possible to remove any fears that the customer might have. It would be reasonable to expect the issue of lead contamination to recede in the future as more producers move towards capsules made of plastic or inert materials or, as in some countries, lead is banned altogether.

This maximizes the surface area of wine in the bottle, making it less prone to fizz up very quickly once opened. Remove the foil and then the wire muzzle and put them away. Once the muzzle is removed there is nothing to stop the cork from suddenly flying out of the bottle, so keep a thumb on the top of the cork from then on. For extra security a napkin wrapped around the bottle and over the neck can ensure that if the cork does escape it will be caught before doing any damage.

With the left thumb over the top of the cork and the 'mushroom' clasped by the fingers, use the right hand gently to twist the bottle. Remember to twist the bottle, not the cork, which can crack it. The cork will quickly begin to ease out and you will feel the pressure of the bottle on the left thumb. Slowly let the cork ease upwards. Rather than letting it come out in an uncontrolled 'pop', let the built-up pressure gently release. If there is wine fizzing up you should have the glass standing by to fill up. This can be given to one of the guests and then the other glasses filled up. It is common not to give the host a glass to taste, but if the wine is bought to celebrate a particular person, give the first glass to them. When first pouring the wine it may well fizz up so much that very little actually gets in the glass. Simply go round the table a second time and fill each glass a little more. Left-handed people should follow the same instructions, simply substituting left for right.

'CORKED' WINE

Contrary to popular opinion, 'corked' wine has nothing to do with the presence of cork in the wine. Any such pieces of cork are harmless, although if they cause offence they can be removed with a clean spoon. 'Corked' wine has an unpleasant smell, often described as 'mouldy' or 'musty'. The most usual culprit for this is 2,4,6,-Trichloroanisole (2,4,6,-TCA), a chemical which at even a few parts per trillion can give a wine a noticeable odour. This develops in corks through the use of hypochlorite, used to bleach corks as part of their production process. Alternatively, certain insecticides or wood treatments (particularly pentachlorophenol PCP) that are used in wineries and cork storehouses can be metabolized by some fungi into 2,4,6,-TCA so that even unbleached corks can produce 'corky' smells. Other than 2,4,6,-TCA various other compounds can produce off odours. These include chloropyrazines, occasionally produced through the boiling and subsequent bleaching of cork slabs, and sulphurous compounds derived from sulphur dioxide, widely used in the wine industry as a sterilizing agent and an antioxidant (Jackson, 1994: 317–18).

To overcome the problem of corkiness in wine, various producers have started experimenting with alternative closure methods and different ways of processing cork. Despite a number of advances, many producers are sticking to traditionally produced cork. Alternative bleaching agents seem to impart their own undesirable aromas and many consumers object to screwtop bottles or synthetic stoppers, particularly on expensive wines.

The number of bottles suffering from some kind of cork derived taint is a subject of debate in the wine industry, not least because taints are not always immediately recognizable, particularly to the untrained nose. Many bottles dismissed as 'slightly woody' may in fact be tainted. Estimates of tainted bottles vary from 2 to 6 per cent, although those selling wine can take some comfort in reports that one major UK wine retailer claimed customers complained about one bottle in 50,000.

As long as sparkling wines have been handled properly they cause few problems. Avoid storing them upright which dries out the corks and makes them prone to breaking. If the cork does break, release the pressure inside the bottle by piercing it and then carefully use a corkscrew to remove the rest. Do not disturb the bottles unnecessarily as this only builds up the pressure inside them. If the cork is particularly stubborn and cannot be removed, a pair of champagne pliers can be used (see 'Corkscrews'), but be careful not to leave the bottle unattended while getting them. Although it may appear jammed in, champagne corks are very unpredictable and it can spontaneously pop out – keep a thumb over the cork at all times.

Dealing with difficult bottles

Occasionally everyone comes across a troublesome bottle that is reluctant to let out its cork or where only half the cork can be pulled out. A wide variety of solutions has been developed to deal with these problems including the following.

- For sticking corks that are hard to pull out, put the neck of the bottle under a warm tap for a few seconds. This should let the glass expand, giving the cork more room and making it easier to remove.
- Where half a cork has broken off and become stuck in the neck, reinsert the corkscrew at an angle and gently pull out.
- Where the cork has crumbled into the wine, use the end of the corkscrew or a spoon handle to lever the pieces out, or in very severe cases use a strainer (preferably silver) and decant the wine.

Perhaps the most troublesome of these problems is where all or half a broken cork has fallen into the wine. Ideally, open a new bottle; salvage methods are clumsy and can be messy. If you do attempt to remove the cork (and in the case of expensive wine it is usually desirable), either decant the wine into a different container, or try to lodge the cork back into the neck where another attempt with a corkscrew can be made.

Skewers can be used to lever the cork back into place for this second attempt but they must be scrupulously clean. Do not use string with a knot in the end to act as an anchor drawing the cork up into the neck – the string cannot be cleaned and is likely to taint or contaminate the wine. There are devices commercially available which act as a claw to grab and pull out the cork. Unfortunately these have a tendency to shatter the glass as they pull the cork into the neck.

Serving wine

The main object is not to drip wine on the table or anyone's clothes. Hold the bottle with the neck over but not touching the glass and pour the wine in, twisting the bottle when finished to stop drips from dropping on the table. Glasses are usually filled two-thirds full, but if the glasses are particularly large then use your discretion. Some restaurants offer the customer a larger glass if they are having a particularly fine wine. The object of this is not to get more in the glass but to allow the wine to be swilled and develop its bouquet in the glass.

The order of service begins from the host's right and goes anti-clockwise around the table. Finally the host has the glass in which the wine was tasted filled up.

Once all the party has been served the bottle is put either in an ice bucket (for white wines) or on the table (for red wines). Increasingly, smaller or more informal restaurants consider ice buckets to be cumbersome, messy and unnecessary. There is a wide variety of wine coolers on the market which keep the wine cool for as long as most tables are likely to want. These coolers have the added advantage of not dripping water all over the table every time the bottle is removed. Their relative cheapness, as well as their size, mean that even in a cramped restaurant one can be provided per table. Ice buckets and stands take up floor space and need to be away from any 'thoroughfares' on the restaurant floor where they might get knocked over. If the restaurant is short on space there is a temptation to use one bucket for two tables. This often puts the bottle out of the reach of one of the tables. Customers are unable to serve the wine themselves which means that staff need to be vigilant that glasses are not getting empty.

Traditionally, red wine is placed in a coaster while on the table. Apart from possibly catching any drips that make their way down the side of the bottle, coasters are fairly useless things. They tend to add to the clutter of a table, and are one more item to be cleaned, stored and forgotten. For restaurants keen to dispel the mystery of wine and make both staff and customers feel rather more relaxed about wine service and consumption, disposing of these tiresome objects could be a good place to start.

How often to refill a person's glass is something that can cause irritation. Most people find it very distracting to have a waiter or waitress hovering over them and refilling their glass after almost every mouthful. Equally, if the wine is not to hand customers can suffer from 'under-service', with empty glasses and no way of filling them themselves. One way to overcome this is to allow a party to fill its own glasses when it feels ready. By leaving red wine on the table and white wine in a cooler or bucket next to the host, they are at liberty to fill their glasses whenever they want. Then it is just a question of keeping an eye on those tables who actually want somebody to come over and fill their glasses.

Once a bottle has been finished, remove it from the table. If the bottle is finished well before the party has finished eating, and using suitable judgement, it is worth discreetly asking the host whether another bottle is required. If they do want another, use a fresh glass for the host to taste the wine before serving it. As long as it is the same wine, there is no need to change the rest of the table's glasses.

Decanting wine

There are two situations when you might want to decant wine. First, when the customer wants the wine decanting, second when the wine needs decanting. The first is more common than the second. Decanting requires a spotlessly clean, dry and odourless decanter, a table light or candle, a funnel and a steady hand.

If a customer asks that a wine is decanted the best thing to do is to oblige. Most wines can withstand decanting. While the process might dull their bouquet and make them a little lacklustre (especially if they are left to 'breathe') it makes very few wines undrinkable. There are instances of very delicate wines that if decanted or left exposed to oxygen can go off very quickly, but these are rare and venerable wines which rarely appear on the wine lists of restaurants. Young wines hardly ever need decanting. Some customers might ask for a

SEDIMENT IN WINE

In the past wine drinkers had to put up with far more solids in wine than we do today. Red wines would stain the bottles they were put in and white wines would leave a very fine deposit known as 'beeswing'. In fact the phenomenon was so well known that those who worked in wine cellars in France would say that there was something to eat as well as something to drink in the bottom of a bottle of wine (Peynaud, 1987: 240). Nowadays technical advances and customer pressure mean that most producers go to great lengths to remove solids from their wine and make efforts to stop them occurring later on. The first group of solids that is removed are the pieces of grape pulp which get left in wine naturally during production. These are left to settle at the bottom of the vat or barrel, although they sometimes need the help of 'fining' agents that clarify the wine. Bentonite (a clay), egg white, gelatine, casein from milk, isinglass derived from fish, tannin made from oak galls and a variety of synthetic materials (such as the tongue twister polyvinylpolypyrrolidone) are all used as fining agents. Because some of these agents derive from animal sources, there are now also 'vegetarian' or 'vegan' wines. Many wines undergo filtration to remove sediment and particles in suspension.

Second, producers may 'stabilize' their wine. For instance, chilling wine over a period of days removes tartrates which can form later. These tartrates are commonly seen as little crystals or flakes on the underside of corks. Although feared by many consumers and taken as a fault, they are quite harmless, the vast majority being cream of tartar (potassium bitartrate). The problem has been exacerbated in recent years as wines from warmer regions of the world, which tend to suffer more from this affliction, have grown in popularity. Consumers have developed a taste for young, early bottled wines that have not had the chance to precipitate these crystals.

While producers go to great lengths to ensure that most table wines have no deposit, those wines that are intended for lengthy ageing must produce a sediment as part of the process. As the wines grow older, phenols such as bitter tannins and anthocyanins (responsible for much of the colour in red wines) polymerize and form into long chains. These eventually become too long to remain in suspension and fall as a sediment onto the bottom of the bottle. This is what decanting leaves behind and can vary from a light dusty sludge in burgundies to sheaves of flaky black sediment in very old ports.

very young wine to be decanted to allow exposure to the air to 'soften' the wine, but in truth this merely removes the wine's vibrancy. Invariably it is the best policy to oblige, but be aware that the wine will not show at its best if it has been left to stand for a time in a decanter – no matter what its age. The only exception to this rule is those wines that have some fault which a brief period in the open can rectify, such as 'bottle stink'. These wines are rare on restaurant lists.

However, some wines do need decanting. These are bottles with a deposit (see box) and are usually red wines over six to eight years old which have plenty of tannin. Wines that do need decanting will have 'thrown' a deposit or sediment. This should be obvious by holding the bottle up to a light where it will appear as a muddy sludge, or as flakes lining the inside of the bottle. Be careful not to move the bottle unnecessarily as this will disturb the sludge and make the wine far harder to decant.

To prevent unnecessary aeration, refrain from decanting until the very last minute, preferably just before the wine is to be served. The cork can be drawn with the bottle either at a slight tilt (so that the sediment remains down the side of the bottle where it has formed as it lay on its side) or standing upright. The cork should only be drawn with the bottle standing upright if the bottle has stood that way for long enough for the sediment to have fallen and settled on the bottom. Draw the cork gently. Corks from old bottles are more likely to be fragile and break. Violent pulling on the cork will stir up the sediment. Then, with a light behind the shoulder of the bottle, start to pour the wine through a funnel into the (spotlessly clean and dry) decanter. The light should allow you to see when the wine passing into the neck of the bottle stops being crystal clear so that you can stop pouring immediately. The pouring motion should be a single action as a stop half-way will mix up the wine and sediment. If possible try to pour the wine so that it trickles down the side of the decanter rather than splashing into the middle. Some decanting funnels have a twisted spout which directs the wine onto the side of the decanter to achieve this.

> Decanting my wine at the last minute, I keep the bottle in the position in which it has slumbered for so long and I decant as much brilliant wine as possible.... Decanting should be done gently: pour slowly, hold the decanter at an angle so that the liquid runs down the insides instead of tumbling in a stream to strike the bottom, which would tire the wine. Watch the clarity across the shoulders of the bottle and, as soon as sediment gathers and begins to be drawn into the clear wine, bring the bottle back up quickly so as to hold it back.
>
> (Edouard Kressman, 1971, cited in Peynaud, 1987: 243)

Wine accessories

Wine, like any pursuit with a passionate group of devotees, has spawned a vast array of gadgets and equipment that supposedly add to its enjoyment. Many wine lovers see these bits and pieces as indispensable, but for those dealing with wine in a professional context they should be treated with some circumspection. Wine accessories are often very expensive and can have a negligible effect on the customers' final enjoyment of the product. Some of the more useful items are listed below, as well as some that restaurants that can manage perfectly well without.

> **THE CHAMPAGNE 'SAUCER'**
>
> The champagne saucer is one of the wine world's great design errors. It was reputedly modelled on the bosom of Marie Antoinette, wife of King Louis XVI of France, using the logic that the most beautiful wine in the world should only be served in the most beautiful shape. Unfortunately this shape is singularly unsuited to the service of sparkling wine. The vast surface area and shallow depth of the wine means that the bubbles form too quickly and dissipate on the surface. Sparkling wine in saucers never really produces the foamy head that characterizes the best wines and soon falls flat.

Glassware

The most important items of glassware are, not surprisingly, the glasses themselves. Although very practical and economical, the Paris goblet is not the ideal wineglass. It is quite small and does not allow for the wine to be swirled around to release its bouquet. Also it is very open at the top, allowing any bouquet that is released to dissipate into the air, rather than being retained and concentrated in the bowl. The ideal multipurpose, day-to-day wine glass is taller with a more tapered bowl. Fine glasses with elegant slim stems may look attractive but are more prone to breakages, so a compromise is necessary between beauty and practicality.

Sometimes a wide range of glasses is advocated with different styles to be used with different wines. The different styles are usually decreed by tradition. Wines from various German regions, Anjou, Provence, and Chianti all have their own style of glass. Really the only wines that do need a different style of glass are champagne and other sparkling wines. These should always be served in champagne 'flutes' which concentrate the bubbles into a foam at the top of the glass.

Whatever glasses are used they should be kept clean. Not only are dirty or badly washed glasses a health hazard but they can also affect the wine in them. Many wines can be attractive to look at, yet the effect is ruined if the glass is dull or watermarked. Glasses should be polished with a clean cloth before they are used. When washing glasses ensure that the correct amount of detergent is used. The use of too much detergent will cause the smell to linger in the bowl, tainting the wine; use too little and the glasses will not get properly cleaned. Once cleaned do not allow glasses to stand unused for too long or store them in damp or dusty places. Glasses soon pick up musty aromas from forgotten back shelves and if stored upright the bowls fill with dust and other detritus.

Decanters

The other item of glassware commonly seen in restaurants is a decanter. When choosing decanters the ones to go for are solid and plain. These let the wine show itself off and are invariably easier to clean and look after. Many decanters come with a stopper. These are the first part to get broken or lost, yet in a restaurant have little practical use. They are best put away and not used.

Cleaning decanters is a problem as they are fiddly and yet need a thorough cleaning regularly. Methods advocated include torn up strips of newspaper (which acts as a scourer) but by far the best method is a brush designed for the purpose. As the brush is on the end of a slightly flexible wire it can get into the most inaccessible corners of the decanter. Use as little detergent as possible to clean decanters and rinse very thoroughly. When cleaning them just before use, do not rinse with very cold water as this can affect the wine (at room temperature).

Corkscrews

As mentioned before, the ideal type of corkscrew to use is one with a worm thread, rather than a gimlet screw. The best are those with a long screw which gives a greater purchase on the cork and makes it less likely to break. Equally, a broad thread makes for a stronger anchorage. In some very dry corks a narrow thread merely bores a hole out of the middle of the cork, making it very difficult to remove.

Deciding what style of extraction method to use depends on practicality and personal preference. For most people by far the best style is the 'waiter's friend'. This corkscrew is effective for the vast majority of corks and yet is one of the smallest and least obtrusive corkscrews, with the advantage that it can be kept in a pocket. Other 'table' style corkscrews are too bulky and can delay wine service, particularly in a busy restaurant.

- **The waiter's friend.** This invariably has a blade on it to cut the foil, as well as an opener for crown capped beer or water bottles incorporated into the foot. The main secret is to ensure that the screw goes down the middle of the cork and that the cork is drawn out vertically so that it does not crack on the side of the bottle.
- **The screwpull.** This is without doubt the easiest corkscrew to use and very rarely fails. The plastic frame sits on the neck of the bottle and then the (very long and broad) thread is screwed into the cork. Then simply continue turning as the screw first enters the cork and gradually extract it in a smooth movement.
- **The butterfly lever.** Commonly seen as a domestic corkscrew, this is rarely suited to restaurant wine service. The screw (usually a gimlet screw) is driven into the cork and as it goes in the two 'butterfly' levers rise up. Once fully inserted the levers are pressed down to bring out the cork.
- **The counterscrew.** Another domestic corkscrew. The bottom counterscrew should be driven home and the wooden or metal frame of the corkscrew placed over the neck of the bottle. Using the top handle screw the thread into the cork. When it is fully inserted, screw the lower lever the other way to extract the cork as it pushes the frame against the neck of the bottle.
- **The butler's friend.** So-called as it allows the cork to be removed undamaged which can then be placed back in the bottle. The technique is complicated and requires some considerable skill, particularly as it can drive

the cork into the bottle. The two prongs are pushed down the sides of the cork using a seesaw motion. Once pushed down the cork is pulled out using a twisting motion. Because it does not pierce the cork this method can be useful with very fragile corks.

Also worth a mention are champagne pliers. These nutcracker-like devices give extra leverage when extracting a particularly stubborn cork.

Left-handed people should look out for left-handed corkscrews which make opening bottles considerably easier.

Miscellaneous accessories

The wine world has developed all manner of tools to help people to enjoy wine more. Some of these can be quite useful in a restaurant, but many are frankly a waste of money.

- **Bottle baskets and cradles.** These enjoy occasional periods in vogue, although this has little to do with their usefulness. Their purpose is to allow those wines which have thrown a sediment, but do not want decanting, to be poured straight from the bottle without disturbing the sediment. By keeping them at a relatively consistent angle the sediment is meant to stay on the bottom of the bottle. Their use in restaurants is usually to complicate and therefore formalize wine service; as such they are best avoided.
- **Coasters.** Initially these were made to accommodate decanters. As well as preventing drops on the decanter from reaching the table, they allowed the decanter to 'coast' down polished tables – hence their name. Over the years various forms have been adopted from the very simple stands to ornate 'decanter wagons' with wheels and carriagework that could be run up and down the table. Unless the bottle is to rest on a polished wooden table and for the sake of a few drops of wine on a tablecloth, anyone wanting to make wine service rather less self-conscious and more relaxed would do well to discard wine coasters.
- **Decanter funnels.** These come in a range of material from stainless steel and silver to plastic and even porcelain. They all do the same job, although some direct the wine down the side of the decanter so that it does not slosh around. These are useful if you decant a great deal of wine and silver plate ones look nice if decanting is done in front of the customer. Some funnels are fitted with a removable strainer that catches any bits of sediment that trickle through when decanting.

THEATRICALITY IN WINE SERVICE

Some of what is mentioned here is also discussed in Chapters 7 and 9. However, it is worth repeating because at the heart of this topic is the problem of overcoming a reluctance on the part of consumers to try new wines and a certain fear that they may get it 'wrong' somehow when they buy wine.

By being relaxed when serving wine you will pass on that demeanour to your customers. If you can talk fluently about the wines on the wine list, tell little stories about them and describe them reasonably well, the customers will begin to trust your advice. It may then be possible to persuade them to be more adventurous and spend more money.

Know the wine list

Anyone who is likely to be asked questions about the wine list should be able to talk confidently about most of the wines it contains. This does not mean they should be able to describe them in minute detail or talk about the subtleties of their production. They should simply be able to tell the customers what they are going to get and possibly some snippet of information about the producer or region.

The two ways of learning about a wine are to taste it and to read or talk about it. Doing the two together is both more pleasurable and more effective. Regular staff tastings allow them to build up their own impressions about different wines. When asked by customers to recommend wines they are then actually able to 'recommend' a wine and not simply say the one they can remember the name of or that they were told to recommend. Second, if the tastings are 'tutored' by either the sommelier or the manager, the tasting of each wine can be accompanied by relevant facts which are far more easily remembered than if they are simply given as a list of 'things to learn' about the wine.

One very effective exercise that anyone can do is to keep a personal tasting log of all wines tasted. The log should be used to make notes on wines tasted at staff tastings and others too. This allows comparison of wines on the list with previous vintages, different producers, regions and winemaking styles. The notes made in this log help when offering advice to customers.

Serve with style

Good knowledge of wine must be backed up with solid service skills. This means practising them as often as possible and not deliberately avoiding opening bottles or leaving it to someone else. The more service skills are practised the more fluent they become. Sommeliers with fluent service skills inspire confidence in their customers and can encourage more adventurous (and more expensive) drinking.

The best wine service is often the least noticed. Staff who lack confidence tend to be clumsy in their actions which will distract a table while their wine is being served.

Smile!

Wine waiters and waitresses and sommeliers have to look happy in their work. So many seem to take the rather outdated attitude that wine is a serious subject and those that work with it must take a sombre attitude. Wine is a fun subject and the whole purpose of wine is that it is there to be enjoyed. Successful wine sales means communicating this sense of enjoyment to the customer.

DEALING WITH DISASTERS

The combination of breakable glass, staining liquids, frenetic restaurant service and the obstacle course that is many restaurant floors means that every so often anyone serving wine will have a bit of a disaster. This can range from splashing red wine on a customer's clothing to corks exploding from champagne bottles. The procedure for dealing with wine service problems should be laid down by the restaurant (in conjunction with those for dealing with similar incidents in the restaurant), but some general guideline are listed below.

- **Don't panic.** This is easier said than done, particularly if you are rather shocked by what has just happened and somebody is shouting at you. But it is always worth just trying to work out exactly what has just happened before doing anything.
- **Apologise.** This is an area which confuses some people who refuse to apologise (although they feel it would be the right thing to do) on the basis that this may be used as an admission of guilt against by them at some later stage. This is not the case and a quick apology can often diffuse a situation before it gets out of hand.
- **Do not do anything which might make matters worse.** In the case of stains on delicate fabrics this could include applying stain removers or similar which make the stain worse.
- **Work out how the accident happened.** A quick post mortem after an accident can highlight where operating procedures need to be changed and training needs to be intensified.

TRAINING IN WINE SERVICE

Wine service is a skill best picked up by working with an expert in a restaurant who can show students the correct way of doing things and pick up on mistakes and give advice as and when they need it.

Wine service skills are also taught on many college and university courses for those who will need the skills in their job or as an exercise during management training. In particular the Hospitality Training Foundation (formerly the Hotel and Catering Training Company) has included wine service in their National Vocational Qualification (NVQ) course in Food and Wine Service. Further details of this and other ways to learn about wine are contained in the next chapter.

QUESTIONS AND EXERCISES

1 Practice opening bottles of wine. If you normally use a 'table' style of corkscrew then have a go with a pocket 'waiter's friend'. Make sure that you cut the foil off cleanly and that the cork is removed neatly with no pieces left in the wine. Check that you are opening it tidily without leaving any bits of foil lying around.

2. Practice opening bottles of sparkling wine. Remember to open it safely by keeping a thumb over the cork at all times once the muzzle has been removed and pointing the cork away from people. As with still wine, ensure that you clear up all bits and pieces as you open the bottle. Practice pouring the wine, watching out for glasses that foam up very quickly.
3. Decant a bottle of wine. If possible do this using a red wine that has deposited a sediment and a clear glass decanter. Otherwise practice using an ordinary red wine and an empty wine bottle. If you use the second method to practice, ensure that you use a light source as if you had to look for the sediment and a funnel.
4. Start a wine tasting book. Use it to make notes on all the wines you try and not just expensive or special bottles. Some people find it easier to work with loose-bound notebooks, record cards or even laptop computers. Often simpler is better, the quality of your notes being more important than the quality of your record keeping.
5. Research your restaurant's wine list (or any other wine list if a student). For each wine make very short notes about where it comes from and any interesting information you can discover. Rewrite this into text you could use to sell the wine to customers remembering:

   - to keep it short;
   - keep it interesting;
   - make it relevant to the sort of customers you serve.

6. Describe the process of wine service from when the customer receives the wine list up to and including the pouring of glasses around the table, explaining the order of service.
7. Why do some wines need decanting and what equipment is needed to decant them?
8. Find two wines that would need decanting. At what stage in their life would they need decanting and for how long could they reasonably be sold from the bottle?
9. Describe what a corked wine is in terms suitable for: a wine 'buff'; someone who likes wine but describe themselves as 'no expert'.
10. Write a standard operating procedure to be given to new waiters and waitresses telling them what to do if they spill wine over a customer.

FURTHER READING

Wine service is covered in the training manuals of the various bodies who offer qualifications in this field. However it is also covered comprehensively in a number of guides. *Food and Beverage Service* by Dennis Lillicrap and John Cousins (1990) covers all aspects of food and beverage service and integrates wine service within the wider framework of the restaurant service process.

The Beverage Book by Andrew Durkan and John Cousins (1995) is in some ways more concise, but also gives useful tips on successful wine service.

Training specialist staff 9

> **Key concepts**
>
> The main concepts covered in this chapter are:
>
> - the sommelier;
> - development of product knowledge and service skills;
> - wine training and education;
> - basic training;
> - intermediate training;
> - advanced training;
> - Master of Wine.

INTRODUCTION

Although sommelier is now a term applied exclusively to wine waiters, the duties of earlier sommeliers were far more varied. At first they were the monks who held responsibility for crockery, bread and linen, as well as wine in monasteries. The term was later applied to staff who received wine from *sommiers*, whose name derives from *bêtes de somme* or beasts of burden (*Larousse Gastronomique*, 1988: 992). The exact nature of the job changed over the years, encompassing responsibility for the king's luggage in transit and even his furniture, eventually becoming the person with responsibility for wines in the houses of the nobility.

THE SOMMELIER

Nowadays the term sommelier is applied to the wine waiter or wine steward in a restaurant. Usually only found as a distinct member of staff in better quality restaurants, the sommelier is often distinguished from the other staff by wearing a slightly different outfit. One of the traditional marks of a sommelier is a *taste-vin*, or traditional wine tasting cup, hung around the neck on a chain.

More often than not this is impractical to wear during service and is retained only to be worn at the meetings of guilds and associations. Instead, the insignia of professional bodies (jackets and pocket or lapel badges) are worn. In the case of junior staff, a black apron with a black 'bum freezer' jacket is worn as opposed to the white apron of the other staff. Many of the examinations leading to membership of the professional associations are extremely demanding and the insignia are worn with considerable pride.

At the risk of overgeneralizing, on the continent this vast knowledge is taken extremely seriously. Within the restaurant hierarchy the sommelier is one of the more senior members of staff, answerable to, if not alongside the head waiter. In some cases the specialist nature of the training may have meant that from an early age the budding sommelier has worked alongside a more senior one who will demonstrate the skills they need to learn. In the closed season the apprentice is given the chance to attend more formal studies at a specialist college. The duties they must learn are not simply confined to the dining room. Many sommeliers are responsible for the selection and ordering of the wines of a restaurant or hotel as well as the management of the cellars. This task may well involve management of a number of junior staff, as well as liaison with other departments such as purchasing and control and finance. These duties clearly make the task of the sommelier far more than one of a waiter who also happens to know a bit about wine. Although few truly great cellars exist in restaurants and hotels today, many of the grander establishments are still expected to have a list that represents most of the world's finest names which involves purchases long in advance of putting the wines up for sale. In turn this creates complex financial questions that a competent sommelier must be capable of addressing.

Bearing in mind the earlier caveat about the risk of overgeneralizing, the situation in the UK is not so promising. Although some of the world's finest sommeliers do work in the UK, their high profile in the wine media together with that of their establishments, does tend to conceal the fact that wine waiters and waitresses are generally non-specialist staff with an interest in wine. Despite the old adage that what they lack in knowledge they make up for in enthusiasm, many of these staff are hopelessly underequipped to administer or create a top quality wine list. This is not just a problem for top quality restaurants (or at least those lacking one of the few really superb sommeliers). The mid-price range of wines is one of the most competitive parts of the UK market. Many restaurants target this level and to make an impact on the customer with such wines requires genuine knowledge and careful management.

DEVELOPMENT OF PRODUCT KNOWLEDGE AND SERVICE SKILLS

Within the UK training to be a sommelier is invariably a blend of formal learning with several bodies that specialize in wine knowledge or service and on-the-job experience. Wine service is a practical skill and while it requires a background knowledge of hard facts, most of the day to day problems encountered on the job can only be learnt by actually dealing with them in real life situations. Most of the courses offered by the various bodies listed below allow for this by offering either day release, evening classes or home study packs. Students on Hospitality Management courses may find that they are able to study wines and wine service as part of their course. However, such courses are designed for prospective managers they will not contain the detail required for a sommelier.

Professional organizations

A number of bodies exists to help those interested in selling and serving wine professionally. Some of these are long established, others more recent. There has been a period of consolidation (for instance, with the Guild of Sommeliers being superseded by the Academy of Food and Wine Service), so it is worth keeping an eye on new developments. In a field such as wine service, where exponents might have little interaction with their peers, membership of a professional body gives at least some degree of contact as well as raising the job's profile.

The wine and spirit education trust (WSET)

With three stages of examinations concentrating on all the world's major wine regions, the courses offered by the WSET have set a benchmark of knowledge by which others are judged. Occasionally criticized for too much attention to the 'Old World' of European producers, the content of the courses is dry and concentrates on assimilating hard facts about regions and styles. The courses have also been criticized by consumer magazines which consider them no fun, with too much emphasis on the examinations at the end. This view does rather miss the point. These courses are designed for those who wish to learn about wine in a professional context where you need plenty of hard facts and up-to-date knowledge. Other courses and bodies may offer a more convivial atmosphere and less factual learning, but that is because the wine is there to be consumed, not sold.

There are three levels of examination offered by the Trust: certificate, higher certificate and diploma. These are discussed in greater detail below but in essence they move from fifty multiple choice questions at certificate, one hundred and a short essay at higher certificate and then a leap in knowledge (and effort) for the challenging diploma. Taken over two years, the diploma is best attempted by those with some sort of regular contact with the wine trade and in conjunction with the day release classes offered at various locations around the country. At the end of each series of classes (one each year) there is a day of examinations involving essays, map questions and a tasting paper. The diploma is awarded after success over the two years. Success in the diploma (usually with a good mark) is a prerequisite for entry to the course leading to the examinations for the Institute of Masters of Wine.

The Academy of Food and Wine Service

The Academy of Food and Wine Service was developed from the Guild of Sommeliers which was established in 1953 and subsequently built up into a number of regional branches. The Guild was eventually disbanded and a new body, the Academy of Wine Service, was established in 1988 'to raise the standard of education and skills in the service of wine in the hotel, restaurant and catering industry' (Bennett, 1993: 23). In many ways this was to balance the emphasis that had previously been given to pure wine knowledge (as provided in the WSET examinations) with practical service skills which at that time could only be learnt on the job. About five years later the Academy widened its emphasis to encompass food service. This was partly due to the fact many of those involved in wine service were also food service staff.

The potential students for the Academy's training are those whose duties include wine service, particularly at NVQ levels two and three. Students work through the syllabus using a pack (either sold to the individual or commercial outlet) that comprises a video, a linked learning guide and reference book, a workbook and telephone support from a instructor with practical experience in the industry. There is an examination and various subsequent levels of membership to the Academy from student through associate and full member to fellow, as well as corporate membership. All grades receive a bimonthly newsletter as well as the option to attend tastings and Academy events.

While successful students and those whose prior qualifications allow them to enter directly into one of the higher grades stay on as members of the Academy, the examination is a useful springboard to move on to the more challenging examinations of the WEST and the Court of Master Sommeliers.

The Hospitality Training Foundation

This training body, formerly known as the Hotel and Catering Training Foundation (HCTC) offers wine service modules as part of its NVQ in Food and Wine Service.

The Court of Master Sommeliers

The syllabus and examinations of the Court of Master Sommeliers, like the WSET, are divided up into various stages of difficulty. The first stage, the Basic Course, is aimed at those doing NVQ levels one and two and covers basic wine knowledge and service skills. There is an examination at the end consisting largely of multiple choice or questions requiring one-line answers. The next level, the Advanced Course, takes place over four days. Three days are taught and one day is taken up with examinations. The course is highly practical and tests with tasting and service skill as well as wine knowledge. The Master Sommelier Diploma is the top level qualification which tests theory, table service in a restaurant setting and tasting skills. The latter is particularly challenging, requiring a 75 per cent pass mark. Increasingly the Court works abroad, particularly in the USA and Australia, where it is assisted by local sommeliers who have already passed the examinations.

The Hotel and Catering International Management Association (HCIMA)

As well as being an international body representing the professional interests of the hospitality industry, the HCIMA is the awarding body for the professional certificate and professional diploma of the HCIMA. Both these courses cover wine to a very limited degree in the food and beverage components and are available at a range of colleges and universities.

The Association also provides a great deal of very useful information for those involved in wine sales through its two-monthly magazine *Hospitality*. Articles range from interviews with members who have tackled wine sales successfully to practical information about new innovations in the industry. In the past, looseleaf 'Briefing Sheets' inserted in the magazine have contained information about legislation and regulations concerning drink sales.

The Young Sommeliers Club of Great Britain

This organization was formed in 1994 and is not an examining body but a tasting club for young sommeliers. The Club is for those already well qualified and established as sommeliers and membership is by invitation only. Regular visits are made to European wine producers and there are frequent meetings in London.

WINE TRAINING AND EDUCATION

A diverse range of bodies has been involved in the process of wine education and training. Their varying aims has meant that there is no immediately apparent structure to the process. Gradually though, as the development of wine skills is brought within the umbrella of vocational training, structure is being imposed upon it. The basics of this structure are reflected in the way in which the remaining sections of this chapter are divided into basic, intermediate, advanced and super advanced training. As with the gradual structuring of vocational training for the drinks industry, at each level there is a mix of 'wine education', the development of product knowledge, and industry training, wine service and management skills.

BASIC TRAINING

The aim here is to introduce those with little or no knowledge of wine or wine service to some very basic concepts and skills. For those who feel they have a reasonable knowledge, picked up over time through observing wine being served or discussing it with friends, particularly those new to the hospitality industry, it is worth going back to the beginning when preparing to deal with wine as a 'professional'. The reason for this is twofold. First, subsequent training is founded on the skills and knowledge learnt at this stage and those who are unsure of certain concepts (for instance in the process of wine production) will find they are at a disadvantage when subsequently they try to build on insufficient or incorrect knowledge.

Second, dealing with wine in a professional capacity is very different from dealing with it in a domestic or hobbyist way. This does not mean that it is any less engaging or fascinating, just that the objectives of the wine professional are to make money out of providing people with the enjoyment of wine, not simply to have that enjoyment themselves. To do this they must approach wine not with the intention of satisfying their own palate but – without prejudice – to satisfy someone else's. By attempting to develop wine knowledge 'knowing what you like', the temptation is simply to concentrate on these areas and risk ignoring others, even though in time they may well be what customers want to buy. Thus confirmed red wine drinkers (as wine lovers) may be tempted to develop their wine knowledge from what they know of red wine, and so alienate their white wine drinking customers through their insufficient knowledge.

The Wine and Spirit Education Trust (WSET) Certificate

For many years now the WSET certificate has been the foundation of professional wine knowledge. Of all the wine courses on offer throughout the UK, this is the one best suited to those who are dealing with wine as part of their job. Academically it is the most rigorous of all the wine courses. This is because much of it is based on the student learning where wines come from and how they are made, with large areas covered in each class. Students are expected to absorb a large number of facts about wine and wine production and so lectures during the course tend to be rather dry and academic. There is little time given over to discussion or development of basic ideas. To qualify for the certificate at the end of the course, students must take a multiple choice examination. Frankly this is not demanding, but the pressure upon many students to pass who have been paid for and sent by their employers, does give the course and examination a certain austerity.

As well as students sent on the course by employers from the on- and off-licensed trade, there are those studying while at college or university and a number of wine enthusiasts. Part of the popularity of this course is that it is run nationwide at a wide range of institutions. This accounts for non-professional wine enthusiasts, for whom the dry, academic nature of the course would seem to be anathema when wine should be about enjoyment. The material covered on the course is contained in several pieces of literature sent out by the Trust about particular regions as well as in the textbook (sent to students and available in bookshops), *The New Wine Companion* by Burroughs and Bezzant (1988). Examination at the end of the course is by multiple choice, with fifty questions to answer in an hour. On examination days, the numbers of students are swelled by those who have covered the syllabus by home study.

Basic wine service skills

For those selling wine in restaurants, merely knowing where wines come from and how they are made is not enough. Good service skills are sometimes forgotten in the rush to develop into a 'wine buff'. This is a pity because a truly good sommelier will combine these two skills and may find that any

> **THE WSET BY HOME STUDY**
>
> As one who has studied (and passed) all the WSET examinations by home study — certificate, higher certificate and diploma — I feel qualified to pass on some advice about this rather challenging route to the qualifications. The material sent to students is identical to that given to those who attend the classes and includes full lists of the wines tasted. For the certificate and higher certificate this is more than adequate as a thorough knowledge of the course textbooks by David Burroughs and Norman Bezzant, *The New Wine Companion* (certificate) and *Wine Regions of the World* (higher), is sufficient for a good pass. Neither of these examinations involves a tasting component, so lengthy practice of tasting exercises is not necessary.
>
> The diploma level is rather more difficult. The leap of knowledge from higher to diploma is a big one, and the learning required is far deeper. The examination essay questions require a thorough knowledge of wine production, marketing and producer regions. As home study students do not benefit from class discussion they must read widely outside the (comprehensive) folder of notes from the Trust. The biggest problem though is the tasting papers. The range of wines tasted on the course means that home study students must have some other method for practising tasting skills and trying a wide range of wines. Even as the manager of a high street wine retailer I found it hard to taste sufficient wines and in both sets of examinations the tasting papers were my weakest.
>
> Finally, anyone thinking of embarking on this route to qualification must be prepared to discipline themselves into setting aside their leisure time for academic study on a regular basis and engaging in a wide range of reading.

holes in wine knowledge can be concealed with a certain panache when it comes to wine service. Actual training in wine service comes from three sources. Vocational courses and qualifications for the hospitality industry will often contain a component in this area, particularly if they are aimed at developing service rather than management skills.

Second, specialist bodies, notably the Academy of Food and Wine Service and the Court of Master Sommeliers, provide training, occasionally within the context of broader vocational qualifications. For those who want a foundation in the skills of wine service, the basic course of the Court of Master Sommeliers and the syllabus of the Academy of Food and Wine Service appear to complement the WSET certificate.

Finally, although never ideal when attempting to learn practical skills, a number of books (including this one) cover the essentials of wine service. Other useful texts are contained in the Bibliography.

Learning basic food and wine combinations

Knowledge of basic food and wine combinations is perhaps the most neglected of the various wine service skills. This is not something that can be learnt out of a book, but is built up over time and with experience. At this stage in the development of someone's wine knowledge it is safest to stick to the conventional rules of food and wine matching. Essentially, this is red wine with dark meats and white wine with white meat and fish. By far the most useful way of developing these skills is by actually trying different foods with different wines. Many restaurateurs would find better wine salespeople in their staff if they were to let them try various combinations for themselves. Equally, it is far easier to remember what not to recommend if you have tasted it yourself.

INTERMEDIATE TRAINING

Intermediate training should build upon what has been learnt above and subsequent experience. While this may sound obvious, it is often not done by those developing their wine skills as a professional. There is often the temptation to bypass the basics and get on with what appears to be more interesting work. But, as pointed out above, this can leave those whose basic knowledge was built around the wines they enjoyed, lacking knowledge when it comes to certain wines they do not particularly like which they are still expected to sell.

The main thrusts of training at this stage are the development of a more detailed knowledge of where particular wines come from and how they are produced, alongside greater proficiency in wine service. Quite often this is accompanied by the development of supervisory skills or a specialist responsibility for wine in a restaurant.

The Wine and Spirit Education Trust Higher Certificate

This rather more challenging examination develops the knowledge learnt during the certificate course. The syllabus concentrates on where particular wines come from and what basic characteristics they possess. Students are also expected to show an understanding of the classification systems of various producer countries and within the EC how they can be compared with one another. The examination, one hundred multiple choice questions and an essay in two hours, demands that students not only recall facts but show they understand them as well.

Delicate, expensive and fine wines

Partly because of the nature of wine connoisseurship, special wines tend to be revered and admired with awe. In restaurants where a wine list contains special wines, only senior or experienced staff are allowed to have anything to do with particular bottles. This is an unfortunate attitude as it tends to make more junior members of staff nervous when they do have to deal with these bottles and more likely to make a mistake.

SOME FOOD AND WINE MATCHING EXERCISES

- It is worth trying a dish with a poorly matched wine and a well-matched one. A good example that could be tried as part of a training programme is pieces of game sausage with a light white or even light red wine, followed by a full bodied red. Alternatively, try red wine with a mildly spicy Szechwan dish followed by an Alsatian Gewürztraminer.
- If a restaurant undergoes a large-scale menu or winelist change, prepare a range of dishes and try them with some likely partners from the wine list. Managers should involve as many of the staff as possible in this process, particularly those who are likely to make recommendations to customers. It is important that the process should be structured and all those involved should make notes as they try the various combinations.
- Try certain foods that almost never match wine of any description. Vinegary foods, even salads dressed with a sherry vinegar dressing, invariably spoil or act in conflict with wine. Chocolate puddings overpower most wines (a wonderful exception here is a number of New World sweet wines made with the 'Orange Muscat' grape). Curries never match wine, but it can be instructive to try a variety of beers and lagers with them.
- As a group exercise compare the taste of wine and water after eating globe artichoke. The majority of people (McGee, 1991: 200) find that wine is spoiled and water tastes sweeter after eating artichokes. This has been blamed on a (possibly genetically determined) sensitivity to a compound called 'cynarin' found in the flesh of the plant. Cynarin appears to heighten most people's sense of sweetness.
- Some 'classic combinations' are not as trustworthy as they seem. Try a range of cheeses with several wines. Although red wine does go well with many cheeses, it makes a poor partner for strong blue cheese and a cheese like Roquefort often goes better with a sweet white wine. Try it.
- Look out for bizarre matches. They can lead to interesting recipe ideas. Sweet Marsala wine with gorgonzola cheese dipped in honey is messy but heavenly.

To overcome this, once the basics of wine service have been mastered, it is important to build upon this knowledge and start practising skills such as decanting and serving expensive bottles. This should be done under the watchful eye of a more experienced member of staff who can then gradually retreat into the background. Over time, as confidence develops, a certain panache can be introduced into wine service which, particularly in the case of expensive wines, is what customers are often unconsciously paying for.

> *The New Wine Companion*
> and
> *Wine Regions of the World*
> **by David Burroughs and Norman Bezzant**
> Although the Bibliography lists various useful items, the importance of these two books for those starting wine training or taking the WSET examinations makes them worthy of special comment. Personally I like them, although I know this is not a universal opinion. The books are dry, fact laden and perhaps most damaging, reflect the prejudices of the 'Old School' of the British wine trade in that they concentrate very heavily on Western Europe. The space they devote to different 'New World' producer nations frequently fails to reflect the varying degrees of importance that they have on the UK (or even world) wine trade. For example, Chile and Argentina receive fairly equal attention. While Argentina is a major world producer its exports are minimal. In contrast the huge impact which Chilean wine exports have had should merit having far greater coverage, both in terms of space and proportion.
>
> The reason I like these books is because a truly comprehensive introduction to the world's producer nations would be prohibitively lengthy and offputting to the newcomer student. The historical seat of quality wine production has generally been in western Europe and while some European nations may have lost their way a little over recent years they still have much to offer students. Equally the development of a good corpus of knowledge in any subject requires students to learn a certain amount of factual information – and this is always dry and a little austere, but worth it in the end.

Theatricality in wine service

Once a solid understanding of wine service has been acquired, coupled with the confidence to deal with most situations, a certain style must be introduced into its presentation. Elsewhere it has been mentioned that customers know that they are paying a great deal more for their wine than they would on the high street. Therefore whoever serves it to them must make them feel that they have received value for money. Customers find it difficult to see the benefit of the various cost centres which result in wine mark-up, so it is up to the member of staff who serves the wine to give them some obvious 'tangible' benefit.

The term 'theatricality' is useful if perhaps slightly misleading because the first 'theatrical' quality that wine service staff need to develop is that of knowing how much 'service' a particular table wants. For instance, in an informal restaurant with large parties of young diners, ebullient, chatty staff telling anecdotes about particular wines will give the customers what they want. But the same style of service would be wholly inappropriate for a couple dining in a quiet, intimate restaurant. In that situation the waiter serving the wine needs to play the part of being 'efficient yet unnoticed'.

The second quality comes in the selling skills of the staff. The biggest hindrance to wine selling is that nobody knows what the wine tastes like until they have bought the bottle and tried it. In Chapter 7 a number of methods for overcoming this problem were discussed. The two main ones are to let the customer try some of the wine before they buy or, alternatively, to give the wine a 'character'. This character comes either from some anecdote about the wine (i.e. Piper-Heidsieck Champagne was Marilyn Monroe's favourite) or the art of creative description. Creative description usually means drawing an allusion between the wine and a particular mental image. I once heard of an expensive bottle of burgundy sold by a wine merchant with the line that 'drinking it is like driving an Aston Martin for an hour'. What he wanted to give the customer was the impression that this wine was luxurious, desirable and gave a fleeting sense of real affluence.

The third part of theatricality is in actual wine service. It is sometimes written that the British decant wine more than the French because they like to make a fuss and be made a fuss of. Well if customers are willing to pay to be made a fuss of then why should restaurateurs begrudge them. Different glasses for different wines, bottles wrapped in crisp napkins, a flourish when the wine is poured, a careful eye on the levels of glasses (and an awareness of whether they would rather be left alone) can all greatly enhance a party's enjoyment of their meal.

Developing customer advice skills

Being able to give advice is naturally a product of growing wine knowledge. However in a restaurant there is a number of things that can be done to develop these skills, particularly as far as the individual wines on the list are concerned. Perhaps the most useful is thoroughly to research the wine list. For each wine discover facts about its producer, region, grape variety/ies, style and history. Sources for this information include the various texts available including general wine primers and books on particular regions. More specific details can often be discovered through the wine merchant or importer who supplied the wine in the first place.

For each wine researched, take notes and perhaps annotate some of them into mini-scripts that can be used as part of wine sales technique. The writing down of information, greatly improves one's powers of recall, particularly late at night or when uninspired to make a particular effort.

Cultivating a personal view of wine

Once a reasonably comprehensive knowledge of wine has been developed, it is time to start indulging personal likes rather more. This may seem to run counter to what was said earlier about keeping personal prejudices out of a professional relationship with wine. The main concern is that prejudices, likes and dislikes formed when learning about wine are not allowed to colour an ability to sell wine successfully. For those who have a little consumer knowledge when they come into working with wine professionally, there is a chance that by not going back to the beginning they will fail to develop the knowledge necessary to sell the wines they do not like. For example, if someone has enjoyed drinking wine for several years but never really enjoyed German wines, the temptation is to ignore them subsequently. However, what they should do is to make the effort to learn about these wines before embarking on more complex learning.

The development of a working knowledge of wines that students do not particularly like puts them in a far better position to defend their prejudices. More importantly they are able to say why they particularly like the wines they do enjoy. There are few things more persuasive than someone who evidently enjoys a wine, encouraging you to buy it. So now that a working knowledge of wines has been achieved, it is time to start deciding which ones are preferred and why. Analyse why you enjoy particular wines, and ask whether you could justify this to the customer – a well-justified enjoyment of a particular wine is a very powerful sales tool.

ADVANCED TRAINING

As with all subjects, most people can develop their knowledge to a certain extent but after a while learning becomes extremely tiresome unless sustained by a real personal interest. While wine is a subject in which many have a passing interest and has the added cachet of a certain snob value, those who want to embark on a programme of advanced study will need to be genuinely interested. Because study at this level really needs to be interest driven and people's interests naturally vary, the areas studied tend to become more diverse at this stage. Advanced wine training tends to develop from the 'core' of the WSET Diploma.

Advanced study involves the development of a detailed knowledge of producer regions of the world and the styles of wine produced, alongside a certain amount of technical knowledge. Those studying at this level would be expected to be in, or moving into, supervisory and management roles.

The Wine and Spirit Education Trust Diploma

The word most often applied to this course is 'challenging'. This perhaps reflects the leap in difficulty from Higher Certificate. The two courses are very different in style and require a different sort of learning from the student.

The course is usually taken over two years. The two papers, A and B, can be taken in either order. This is usually dictated by which one is being studied at the institution in the year the student enrols. The course material is copious and contained in ring binders. The introductory page of each year's binder stresses that the material contained is not enough for a student to pass but should serve as a guide for further reading and study. The main problem, particularly for home study students, is that there are few easily accessible textbooks like *The New Wine Companion* and *Wine Regions of the World*. Information has to be drawn from a wide range of books which are really aimed at avid consumers. Many of these are listed in the Bibliography.

As well as theoretical learning the Diploma involves the development of tasting skills. The only way to do this is, not surprisingly, by tasting frequently. Again this provides a problem for home study students as they do not get the benefit of wine tastings in class. The examination, taken after each year, consists of three papers in a day. Written papers in the morning and afternoon are split by a tasting paper, which consists of three unspecified wines and three partially specified wines. The emphasis is on using the correct process in tasting the wine rather than simply guessing what it is.

Basic oenology

Oenology is an imprecise term that is applied to mean anything to do with wine. In practice it has usually meant the study of 'winemaking', from the delivery of grapes to the winery to the bottle on the shelf. Increasingly it is applied to the whole process, including 'viticulture', the science of growing grapes in the vineyard.

Sometimes people question whether those involved in selling wine in restaurants have any need to study processes and techniques that are far removed from it and in which they will have very little involvement. Wine connoisseurship is a curious art however. Although the information learnt through studying oenology may not be very useful, it can appear impressive and make customers confident to choose wines because the waiter or sommelier is an 'expert'. Knowledge of production methods allows the sommelier to explain (in reassuringly technical terms) why one wine tastes different from another.

There are training courses for those who wish to become full-time oenologists, but these are mostly in universities or colleges in producer nations. For those who wish to develop their knowledge in this field without going to the trouble of studying full time, subscriptions to wine magazines and looking out for interesting books is more than sufficient. Several of these books are listed in the bibliography.

Wine faults

One of the most useful aspects of learning something of oenology is that it helps to understand some of the reasons why wine goes 'off'. Wine is a living product and not all bottles will necessarily end up the same. There is an old French phrase that 'there are no great wines, only great bottles'. Any career spent dealing with wine is bound to encounter a few bad bottles along with the great ones. Over time as students of wine taste more bottles they will gradually come up against a few that have some sort of fault. While this may sound strange, you should revel in these bottles (although hard to do when it involves a particularly expensive bottle of burgundy that you have been looking forward to for weeks). Only by tasting faulty bottles can you recognize them in the future, particularly if the fault is not so obvious or detectable.

> **THE WINE BORE**
>
> This term can apply to overzealous sommeliers as much as to archetypal crusty colonels holding forth over a bottle of claret. The possession of a great wine knowledge can be a very useful sales tool and some customers actively seek restaurants where the sommelier can talk at great length about the wines on the list. Equally, many customers would run a mile if they thought they were going to be faced with a sommelier who told them about production methods and volatile acidity.
>
> Elsewhere in this book it has been said that selling skills are a matter of getting a 'feel' for what level or style of service a particular party wants. Some like to be given punchy anecdotes about wine and amusing stories with a light-hearted tone. Others want someone who can tell them what grape varieties are involved in a wine's production, that it was barrel fermented, that the barrels were French, that it is a wine with a very limited production. Some just want a bottle of house white and to be left alone.
>
> So while I would recommend any budding sommelier to try and build up their wine knowledge, they should be sparing and sensitive to customers' desires when it comes to letting the world know what they have learnt.

There are three important factors when dealing with faulty bottles in a restaurant. The first is correctly to recognize it. This means knowing the difference between 'bottle sickness' or 'stink' and a genuinely faulty bottle. Bottle sickness can have a number of causes but disappears within a few minutes or after a bottle has been decanted. Similar smells can also be caused by wine being opened too soon after bottling, when traces of sulphur dioxide used to prevent oxidation during bottling, are still obvious. These gradually disappear over time but are a fault of the merchant for selling wine that is unready to drink. Finally, smells like this may be permanent and from a variety of sources, not least the cork. Although unavoidable, good merchants will refund these bottles. Knowing the difference between these three types of fault is something that needs experience.

Once a bottle has been identified as faulty it should not be treated as some sort of oddity (which unfortunately it isn't) but as just an everyday occurrence. Finally it should be replaced without question and returned to the wine merchant. Inexperienced staff often do not feel as though they possess the authority to deal with a problem like this and so hand it over to someone more senior. With faulty wine in particular managers must make staff feel as though they will have the full backing of management, no matter what action they take.

MASTER OF WINE

The letters MW after a person's name rightly engender a certain amount of respect in the wine trade. The examination was initially set up by several wine merchants and The Vintners' Company to give the trade a very demanding qualification, equivalent to those found in other professions. The first examination was taken by 21 candidates in London in 1953 and only six passed. In recent years the number of successful candidates has exceeded 200, still a minute proportion of those who attempt the three days of papers. The examination has always been the same, involving five written papers and three tasting papers. Examination centres have also been set up in New York and Sydney for overseas candidates who have been allowed to take the examination since 1987. The written papers cover material from throughout the world on wine production, marketing, transport, quality control, and many other subjects. The tasting papers require a vigorously analytical approach and can require candidates to spot faults and identify specific wines.

In the early years preparation for the examinations was very much left up to the individual candidate. Now there is a mandatory education programme that involves trips to producer regions with other candidates and lectures or workshops with successful Masters. One of the strengths of the governing body, The Institute of Masters of Wine, has been the willingness of its members to give their expertise to those who aspire to join.

Wine cellar management

One of the duties that often falls to sommeliers and their teams is that of managing a restaurant's wine cellar. By this stage in a sommelier's training they are more than adequately qualified to know what sort of conditions wine should be kept in. Moreover, one would hope that their employers would have given them the responsibility for choosing and purchasing the wine at least to some degree, even if they had come up through the ranks. Staff who show enough interest in wine to develop their knowledge to the WSET level or equivalent should be rewarded with responsibility for a product on which they are obviously keen.

The sort of work involved in managing the cellar extends from major tasks perhaps undertaken once a year, through to mundane daily tasks of good management. Annual tasks may well involve adjusting the wine list to account for changes in what is available, changes to the menu or even changes in what is good value. While responsibility for the cellar is often a rather pleasant task, it also involves the not so glamorous duties of stocktaking, cleaning, ordering and shifting cases once they have been delivered. In larger outlets there is also a responsibility for training more junior members of staff.

SUPER ADVANCED TRAINING

Wine has always been viewed in a curiously technical light by the English-speaking world and this is reflected in the sort of training which is offered to those who wish to take their knowledge further. In the UK and increasingly worldwide, the ultimate qualification for those who are not wanting a technical qualification in wine 'production' is Master of Wine (see box). The very demanding nature of this qualification, the preparation time needed and the fact that both students and employers must make sacrifices if hopeful candidates are to have a reasonable chance with the examinations, mean that few in the restaurant business have the opportunity to study for it.

Other than the examinations for Master of Wine there is little else that those in English-speaking countries can do to develop their knowledge, particularly if they are not to become wine producers or work with wine in a technical capacity. This contrasts with countries such as Italy where colleges run courses in the skills of the sommelier. The reasons for this are unclear, although certainly the attitude to wine and those in hospitality occupations in Britain may well contribute. Wine connoisseurship has long been seen as the skill of the consumer, not the staff. Those who drank wine were once in the minority. Throughout the world, quality wine has become increasingly popular and an elitist attitude is no longer acceptable. The idea that wine and wine service are not subjects fit for academic and vocational study does the consumer a grave disservice.

QUESTIONS AND EXERCISES

1. The most useful exercise for those wanting to develop their wine skills and knowledge requires only a wine list and a reasonable library or basic wine guide. Using preferably your own or your restaurant's wine list, try to research as much as you can about the wines. For each wine make a series of bullet points or short notes. These should include where it comes from, what grape varieties are used, who the producer is, and anything else you think useful or interesting.

   From this information devise short scripts you could use to sell this wine to customers giving three different scripts per wine, one each for:

   - a 'wine buff' you know, who likes to be told technical information;
   - a jolly table of twenty-somethings;
   - a romantic couple.

   Finally, using the descriptions, decide which wines you could best sell to which of the three parties.
2. At what stage in their careers might you expect to put staff through the Certificate, Higher Certificate and Diploma of the Wine and Spirit Education Trust?
3. Find out for yourself what organizations operate in your area that might be able to help your career in professional wine service.

4. As a group try to find out the strangest food and drink (not necessarily wine) combinations that you and your colleagues regularly enjoy. Try and understand why these foods and drinks go together.
5. Establish a reasonably regular evening when you and a group of friends/colleagues get together with a bottle or two of wine. Try to buy wines that are better than what you might normally drink, and discuss what you think of the wines. Make notes and compare a number of wines against each other.

FURTHER READING.

Wine service skills beyond those described in Chapter 8 can really only be learnt from experience and the influence of older, more experienced staff. However, the true test of skill for highly trained, specialist wine staff is their product knowledge. The two finest textbooks for introducing students to the vast range of wine styles are undoubtedly *The New Wine Companion* (1988) and *Wine Regions of the World* (1988), both by David Burroughs and Norman Bezzant.

For more detailed reading on specific regions there is obviously a huge range of books. However, in terms of giving specialist wine staff useful information the Faber and Faber series (described in the next chapter) is invaluable.

10 Wine books and periodicals

INTRODUCTION

This list is by no means exhaustive and is based purely on what is obtainable in UK bookshops and is limited to those books that might be of particular use to anyone involved in selling wine. Where books have been particularly praised, this is because they have been found to be particularly useful or interesting. In Asa Briggs' history of the Victoria Wine Company, *Wine for Sale* (1985), he referred to a comment made by Auberon Waugh a year earlier in the *Daily Mail*, 'that production of books about wine had outstripped even the growth in wine consumption' (p174). This remains true to the present day when books about wine, from the nondescript to the outstanding, fill booksellers' shelves. Many of these can be a worthwhile investment. However, caution is needed to avoid those that are merely repetitive or sell through a novel format or association with a celebrity winetaster. These books are all aimed at consumers. While it is important for a 'wine professional' to understand what the market wants, the most hyped wines in these guides will be the ones with the least available mark-up. The books displayed in boxes are particularly recommended.

BOOKS

The Great Vintage Wine Book II, Michael Broadbent (1991)

This comprises a superb collection of tasting notes of individual wines built up by Michael Broadbent over the years. As with so many wine books, it provides a fascinating read and superb 'cheat sheet' if you know you are to be given something special at a dinner party. The price is expensive (around £30.00) and the book is of limited practical use to a restaurateur unless the wine list contains some real 'greats'. One way to use such books is to display them as a miniature 'wine library' in the cocktail bar or similar for customers to read.

Pocket Guide to Wine Tasting, Michael Broadbent (1992)

One of a range of books on different aspects of wine published in a rather useful pocket size by Mitchell Beazley. Written by one of the first 'Masters of Wine', head of Christie's Wine Department, and author of a number of wine books, this has become something of a wine classic. Very easy to read and packed with useful information it explains why wines taste how they do, what different tastes mean, and how adequately to describe the taste of wine. It also covers how to look after wine and serve it so that it shows its best.

Pocket Guide to Wine Vintages, Michael Broadbent (1992)

This is another useful little Mitchell Beazley wine book listing the characteristics and keeping potential of vintages from regions around the world. It concentrates on the traditional regions of France and Europe – not surprisingly as this is where most of the more usually found older wines come from. For the restaurateur this guide makes a useful reference if buying wines from these classic regions and from good years and can help to avoid buying duff wines. If stocking a simple list of ready-to-drink, easy styles, the book makes an interesting read with notes on wines as far back as the 1890s.

The World Atlas of Wine, Hugh Johnson (1985)

This is probably the most important book on wine in English in the world, and to be found in every wine lovers library. Each chapter covers a small region of wine production, with a description, a selection of wine labels, a photograph or two, and, most importantly, a very detailed map showing exactly where the various vineyards are. It is easy to go on for some time about this book – it is easier simply to say 'buy it'.

Hugh Johnson's Wine Companion, Hugh Johnson (1991)

This exhaustive text is the sister volume to the outstanding *World Atlas of Wine*, also by Johnson. The book describes the major (and many not so major) wine-producing regions of the world and then lists, in varying levels of detail, the important producers in the region. Special features on particular characters and introductory chapters on grape varieties, vineyards and wine production make this book hard to put down and an invaluable reference.

The Taste of Wine (Le goût du vin), Emile Peynaud (1987)

This is a classic on the subject of wine tasting and the sensory evaluation of wines. Every aspect of tasting wine is covered exhaustively, from what you need to how to do it. The book includes some fascinating tasting exercises used on the University Tasting Diploma from the Bordeaux Institute of Oenology where Peynaud was director and co-founder. This book is not included among those particularly recommended for a variety of reasons. Michael Broadbent's *Pocket Guide to Winetasting* (1992) is both more readily available and accessible to the ordinary reader. While Peynaud's writing style and Michael Schuster's translation do everything to make this an entertaining read, the incredible detail with which the subject is treated can at times make the book heavy going.

> *The Oxford Companion to Wine*, Jancis Robinson (ed.) (1994)
>
> This is the ultimate wine book containing over a thousand pages of erudite and fascinating information about every aspect of wine from the earliest stages of production to consumption, history, regions, and paraphernalia. With contributions from perhaps the most outstanding panel of wine experts ever brought together, and well edited by Jancis Robinson, who has written a large number of the entries herself, it is hard to imagine how this sort of text could be improved upon, bar occasional new editions to keep up to date. This is well worth the hefty price tag of around £30.00 at the time of writing.

Faber Books on Wine, General Editor: Julian Jeffs

- *Bordeaux*, David Peppercorn (1991)
- *Burgundy*, Anthony Hanson (1982)
- *French Country Wines*, Rosemary George (1991)
- *German Wines*, Ian Jamieson (1991)
- *Italian Wines*, Philip Dallas (1988)
- *Port*, George Robertson (1992)
- *Sherry*, Julian Jeffs (1992)
- *Spirits and Liqueurs*, Peter Hallgarten (1991)
- *The Wines of Portugal*, Jan Read (1991)
- *The Wines of Greece*, Miles Lambert-Gocs (1991)
- *The Wines of the Rhône*, John Livingston-Learmouth and Melvyn C. H. Master (1991)
- *The Wines of Spain*, Jan Read (1991)
- *The Wines of Australia*, Oliver Mayo (1991)

I hope I can be excused for putting this outstanding series of wine books into this chapter in toto. However, for those who want to gain an in-depth knowledge of a particular wine region no series can compare. The actual format of the books changes from book to book. Some carry details of many different producers while others take a more general approach with discussions of production methods and the region.

PERIODICALS

DECANTER

'The world's best wine magazine' is published monthly, with contributions from its own team of writers as well as from many other highly respected figures from the world of wine. All aspects of wine are covered and it is particularly strong on coverage of the world's classic producer regions. Each issue commonly contains a buying guide of wines tasted by respected trade figures, a comparative tasting of a particular region or vintage, and a number of special features on regions' producers.

Michael Broadbent's monthly Tasting Notes are enjoyed by many *Decanter* readers for their fascinating look into the world of this top wine taster and auctioneer. Perhaps this is the closest to a Fantasy Football League for the wine taster. Annual subscription is currently £35.40 and *Decanter* is available from:

Decanter Subscriptions
120–126 Lavender Avenue
Mitcham
Surrey CR4 3HP

Tel: 0181 646 6672
Fax: 0181 648 4873

Wine magazine

When asked to compare *Decanter* with its only real rival, *Wine*, I have said that they have similar contents, but a markedly different style. Where *Decanter* is sometimes austere and factual, *Wine* magazine adopts a more reader-friendly style. Both cover every type of wine from cheap and cheerful everyday glugging wine to the latest record breakers at auction. *Wine*'s question and answer pages are very useful and they have a summary of latest wines to come to market which often contains some real gems.

Having read both magazines for some time, I have come to the conclusion that perhaps the tasting panels of *Wine* are a little more egalitarian, although whether that makes them any better at picking good wines is another question. For the restaurateur, *Wine* like *Decanter* regularly features restaurants that have good wine lists and these articles can be helpful for tips. However, perhaps its most useful feature is the annual International Wine Challenge, a competitive tasting of thousands of wines, the results of which are published in the magazine in the autumn.

The annual subscription to Wine is currently £35.95 (12 issues) and it is available from:

Wine
PO Box 219
Woking
GU21 1ZW
Tel: 01483 776345
Fax: 01483 776573

SPYGLASS

This is not a wine magazine in the glossy mould of *Decanter* and *Wine*, but a mail order only bulletin. Concentrating on budget wines, the magazine features those from all the major chain merchants and supermarkets as well as a number of better known mail order and independent wine merchants. Its writing style is witty and rather iconoclastic with each issue running features such as 'Legendary Drinkers', gossip in 'One Over the Eight', 'Merchant of the Month' and 'Worst Delivery Award'. Like the other magazines it is primarily aimed at keen wine consumers, but remains a very interesting read. The annual subscription is currently £22.50 (12 issues). *Spyglass* is available from:

Spyglass
NH Publishing
Downside House
Shepton Mallet
Somerset BA4 4JL

Bibliography

Barr, A. (1988) *Wine Snobbery: An Insider's Guide to the Booze Business*,. Faber and Faber, London.
Barr, A (1995) *Drink*, Bantam Press, London.
Barr, A. and Levy, P. (1984) *The Official Foodie Handbook*, Ebury Press, London.
Bennett, J. (1993) 'The development of the Academy of Wine Service', *International Journal of Wine Marketing*, 5 (1), 23–29.
Briggs, A. (1985) *Wine for Sale: Victoria Wine and the Liquor Trade 1860 – 1984*, The University of Chicago Press, Chicago.
Broadbent, M. (1991) *The Great Vintage Wine Book II*, Mitchell Beazley, London.
Broadbent, M. (1992) *Michael Broadbent's Pocket Guide to Winetasting*, Mitchell Beazley, London.
Broadbent, M. (1992) *Michael Broadbent's Pocket Guide to Wine Vintages*, Mitchell Beazley, London.
Brook, S. (1987) *Liquid Gold: Dessert Wines of the World*, Constable, London.
Burroughs, D. and Bezzant, N. (1988a) *The New Wine Companion*, Heinemann Professional Publishing, London.
Burroughs, D. and Bezzant, N. (1988b) *Wine Regions of the World*, Heinemann Professional Publishing, London.
Butler, R. and Walkling, G. (1986) *The Book of Wine Antiques*, Antique Collectors Club, Woodbridge.
Buttle, F. (1986) *Hotel and Food Service Marketing: A Managerial Approach*, Cassell, London.
Campbell-Smith, G. (1967) *Marketing of the Meal Experience: A Fundamental Approach*, University of Surrey, Guildford.
Cracknell, H. and Nobis, G. (1985) *Practical Professional Gastronomy*, Macmillan, Basingstoke.
Dallas, P. (1988) *Italian Wines*, Faber & Faber, London.
Davis, B. and Stone, S. (1991) *Food and Beverage Management*, Butterworth-Heinemann, Oxford.
Douglas, M. and Nicod, M. (1974) 'Taking the biscuit: the structure of British meals', *New Society*, 30 (637), 744–7.

The Drink Pocket Book 1996, NTC Publications in association with Stats MR, Henley-on-Thames.

Driver, C. (1983) *The British at Table*, Chatto & Windus, London.

Durkan, A. and Cousins, J. (1995) *The Beverage Book*, Hodder & Stoughton, London.

Fattorini, J. (1994a) 'Food journalism: a medium for conflict?', *British Food Journal*, 96 (10).

Fattorini, J. (1994b) 'Professional consumers; themes in high street wine marketing', *The International Journal of Wine Marketing*, 6 (2).

Finkelstein, J. (1989) *Dining Out: A Sociology of Modern Manners*, Polity, Cambridge.

Floyd, K. (1988) *Floyd in the Soup*, Pan, London.

George, R. (1991) *French Country Wines*, Faber & Faber, London.

Green, E. (1995) 'Will it be the house red for you, sir?', *Independent*, 23 May.

Grigg, C. (1995) *Wine Magazine*, 10 (4).

Hallgarten, P. (1991) *Spirits and Liqueurs*, Faber & Faber, London.

Hanson, A. (1982) *Burgundy*, Faber & Faber, London.

Hanson, A. (1995) *Burgundy* (Second edition), Faber & Faber, London.

Jackson, R. (1994) *Wine Science: Principles and Applications*, Academic Press, San Diego.

Jacobs, E. and Worcester, R. (1990) *We British: Britain under the Moriscope*, Weidenfeld and Nicolson, London.

Jamieson, I. (1991) *German Wines*, Faber & Faber, London.

Jeffs, J. (1992) *Sherry*, Faber & Faber, London.

Johnson, H. (1985) *The World Atlas of Wine*, Mitchell Beazley, London.

Johnson, H. (1989) *The Story of Wine*, Mandarin, London.

Johnson, H. (1996) *Hugh Johnson's Pocket Wine Book*, Mitchell Beazley, London.

Johnson, H. (1991) *Hugh Johnson's Wine Companion*, Mitchell Beazley, London.

Johnson, H. (1985) *The World Atlas of Wine*, Mitchell Beazley, London.

Ladenis, N. (1987) *My Gastronomy*, Headline, London.

Lambert-Grocs, M. (1991) *The Wines of Greece*, Faber & Faber, London.

Larousse Gastronomique, (1988) Paul Hamlyn, London.

Lillicrap, D. and Cousins, J. (1990) *Food and Beverage Service*, Hodder & Stoughton, London.

Livingston-Learmouth, J. and Master, M. C. H. (1991) *The Wines of the Rhône*, Faber & Faber, London.

Loftus, S. (1985) *Anatomy of the Wine Trade*, Sidgwick & Jackson, London.

McGee, H. (1991) *On Food and Cooking: The Science and Lore of the Kitchen*, HarperCollins, London.

Mayo, O. (1991) *The Wines of Australia*, Faber & Faber, London.

Neill, R. (1996) 'The art of wine and seduction', *Decanter*, 12 (5).

Parker, R. (1989) *The Wine Buyers Guide*, Dorling Kindersley, London.

Peppercorn, D. (1991) *Bordeaux*, Faber & Faber, London.

Peynaud, E. (trans. M. Schuster) (1987) *The Taste of Wine*, MacDonald, London.

Read, J. (1991) *The Wines of Portugal*, Faber & Faber, London.
Read, J. (1991) *The Wines of Spain*, Faber & Faber, London.
Robertson, G. (1992) *Port*, Faber & Faber, London.
Robinson, J. (1986) *Vines, Grapes and Wines*, Mitchell Beazley, London.
Robinson, J. (ed.) (1994) *The Oxford Companion to Wine*, Oxford University Press, Oxford.
Slattery, P., Feehely, G. and Savage, M. (1996) *A Golden Age for Hospitality: Share Valuation Overview*, Kleinwort Benson Research, London.
Unwin, T. (1991) *Wine and the Vine*, Routledge, London.
Veblen, T. (1899) *The Theory of the Leisure Class* (originally published by Macmillan, New York) Dover, New York.
Wood, R. (1994) *Organizational Behaviour for Hospitality Management*, Butterworth-Heinemann, Oxford.

Index

Academy of Food and Wine Sevice, 139, 140, 143
accessibility, 106
agents, 61–2
Airén, 47
appeal, 106
Appellation d'Origine Contrôlée (AOC), 89
ASDA, 106
auctions, 59
Australia, 4, 26, 27
Australian Liqueur Muscats, 112

bar equipment, 63
basic training, 141–144
basic wine service skills, 142
beer, 23, 24
bin cards, 74
bin ends, 110
bin numbers, 89
blackboards, 78
blind tasting, 51
bottle baskets and cradles, 133
bottle sickness, 150
bottle sizes, 113
bottle stink, 130, 150
brand, 31
Britain, 3

British Wine, 22
brokers, 59
Bulgaria, 26, 27
bulk discounts, 65
Burgundy, 31
buying wine, 41
by-the-glass technology, 108, 115

Cabernet Sauvignon, 14, 43, 112
carafes and jugs, 114
cellar stock ledger, 74
Chablis, 80
chalk boards, 118
champagne, 18, 28, 31
champagne flutes, 131
champagne pliers, 124
champagne saucer, 131
Charbono, 51
Chardonnay, 14, 15, 31, 48, 112
    from Australia, 80
Chianti, 31
Chile, 14, 15, 50
choice, 71
christmas, 109, 112
Claret, 31
class, 7, 12, 25, 27, 53
classification, 54, 89
coasters, 133

conservatism and customers, 103
consumer attitudes to wine prices, 82–83
corked wine, 126
corkscrews, 123, 132
    butler's friend, 132
    butterfly lever, 132
    counterscrew, 132
    screwpull, 132
    waiter's friend, 132
cost, 72
cost plus pricing, 80
Court of Master Sommeliers, 140, 143
credit, 66
Culture of Informal Rewards, 70
Côte-Rôties, 44

decanters, 125, 131
    cleaning, 132
    funnels, 133
decanting wine, 128–130
delivery, 66
Denominación de Origen (DO), 90
Denominazione di Origine Controllata (DOC), 90
Denominazione di Origine Controllata e Garantita (DOCG), 90
descriptions, 91
dessert wines, 108
difficult bottles, 127
disasters, 135

Eastern Europe, 4, 14, 50
en primeur, 59
English wine, 22
equipment, 67
European Union, 58
expert and celebrity endorsements, 118–119

fame, 55
fashion, 11, 52
female, 25
financing, 94
fine wines, 144

food, 10, 11
food and wine matching, 144–145
foodie, 10
France, 4, 17, 26, 27

Germany, 17, 26, 27
Gewürztraminer, 43
glassware, 44, 63, 67, 131
goods received, 73
grape varieties, Arién, 47
    Cabernet Sauvignon, 14, 43, 82, 112
    Charbono, 51
    Chardonnay, 14, 15, 31, 48, 83, 112
    Columbard, 83
    Gewürztraminer, 43
    Marsanne, 112
    Muller-Thurgau, 14
    Nebbiolo, 112
    Petit Syrah, 51
    Pinot Noir, 14
    Riesling, 15
    Sauvignon Blanc, 14
    Shiraz, 82
    Tarrango, 51
    Viognier, 51
grapie, 10
grid group analysis, 77
gross profit, 81
Guild of Sommeliers, 139

Harper's, 62
Harper's Trade Directory, 61
Harper's Wine and Spirit Gazette, 99
Harvey's 'Club', 29
history, 5
Hospitality Training Foundation, 140
Hotel and Catering International Management Association (HCIMA), 141

Imperial Preference System, 58
Institute of Masters of Wine, 139, 151

Index

Italy, 4, 17, 26, 27

Jacob's Creek, 30

Koonunga Hill Shiraz/Cabernet, 82

larger bottle sizes, 114
lead and wine, 125
Liebfraumilch, 33
luxury product, 24

Made Wine, 22
magnum, 114
mark-up, 9, 16, 18, 80, 82
    high, 71
market orientated pricing, 80
marketing research, 96–100
marketing wine, 67, 83
Marsanne, 112
Master of Wine (MW), 13, 151, 152
meal experience, 9, 88
men, 25, 26, 28
menus, 91
merchandising year, 112
merchants, 49
methods of pricing, 80
Muller-Thurgau, 14

name of a wine, 30
names, 89
Nebbiolo, 112
New World, 4
New Zealand, 14, 50
newspapers, 12, 26
nitrogen blankets, 117
négociant-éleveur, 59

oenology, 149
Off-Licence News 62
off-licences, 6
off-sales book, 77
opening bottles, 123
opening sparkling wine, 124–126
order of service, 87
oxygen, 116

Paris goblet, 131
Parker, Robert, 55
performance measures, 77–9
periodicals, 154, 157–158
Petit Syrah, 51
pilfering, 70
Pinot Noir, 14
point of sale (POS) material, 107
Portugal, 50
predicting volumes, 63
presenting the bottle, 123
presenting the list, 122
preservation methods, 116
prestige wines, 79
price points, 82
pricing policy, 80, 81–83
producers, 60
product knowledge, 138–139
pudding wines, 108

Qualitätswein bestimmter Anbaugebiete (QbA), 90
Qualitätswein mit Prädikat (QmP), 90
quantity, 66

radio, 12
Redcliff's Colombard Chardonnay, 83
restaurant's image, 79
restaurants, 8
    specialist, 92
returns, 76
Riesling, 15
Rioja, 31

Sauvignon Blanc, 14, 15
sediment, 129
sensory domination, 106
service skills, 138
serving wine, 127
setting merchandising objectives, 105
sherry, 29
snobbery, 30, 34
sommelier, 11, 137
South Africa, 4

Index

Spain, 4, 26, 27
special offers, 109
special purchases, 110
staff, endorsements, 119
    sales book, 77
    training, 10, 11, 12
    wine knowledge, 95
stock control system, 73
storage, 94
Super Tuscans, 54
supplier policy, 67
suppliers, 72

Tarrango, 51
tastings, 17, 42, 44, 67, 155, 155
    appearance, 45
    panels, 99
    smell, 45
    taste, 46
    terms, 42
television, 12, 29
tent cards, 78, 107
The Drink Pocket Book, 99
theatricality, 133, 146
transfer book, 76
Trebbiano, 47
tutored tasting, 111

ullage book, 76
USA, 4

vacuuming, 117
VAT, 17, 18
Vins délimité de qualité supérieure (VDQS), 89
vintage, 90
Viognier, 51
Volnay, 11

vulnerablilty of wine, 72

wholesalers, 62
wine accessories, 130
Wine and Spirit Educational Trust (WSET), 12, 13, 139
    Certificate, 12, 13, 142
    Diploma, 12, 13, 148
    Higher Certificate, 12, 13, 144
    home study, 143
Wine and Spirit International, 62, 99
wine bore, 150
wine cellar management, 151
wine choice, 33
wine colour preferences, red, 28
    rosé, 28
    white, 28
wine consumption, 21
wine faults, 149
wine list inserts, 78
wine list, length, 93
    writing, 88
wine merchandising, 104–106
wine merchant, 6, 59
Wine of Fresh Grape, 22
wine of the month, 109
wine on tap, 114
wine profitability, 78
wine requisitions, 74
wine books, 154
women, 26, 28
WSET *see* Wine and Spirit Educational Trust, 13

Young Sommeliers Club of Great Britain, 141